putting up

Hot Pepper Jelly
7/21/06

putting up

A Year-Round Guide to Canning in the Southern Tradition

Stephen Palmer Dowdney

Photographs by Rick McKee

Gibbs Smith, Publisher
TO ENRICH AND INSPIRE HUMANKIND
Salt Lake City | Charleston | Santa Fe | Santa Barbara

First Edition
12 11 10 09   5 4 3 2

**Home-canned products may cause serious harm if put up improperly.
As a safety precaution, every recipe in this book must be carefully read,
and the instructions followed accordingly. The recipes and information
in this book have been tested to ensure accuracy. Gibbs Smith, Publisher,
and the author assume no responsibility for any damages, losses or
injuries incurred during the use of this book or the consumption of
products canned following its directions.**

Published by
Gibbs Smith, Publisher
P.O. Box 667
Layton, Utah 84041

Orders: 1.800.835.4993
www.gibbs-smith.com

Designed by Debra McQuiston
Printed and bound in Hong Kong

Library of Congress Cataloging-in-Publication Data
Dowdney, Stephen Palmer.
  Putting up : a year-round guide to canning in the Southern tradition /
Stephen Dowdney ; photographs by Rick McKee. — 1st ed.
     p. cm.
 ISBN-13: 978-1-4236-0280-4
 ISBN-10: 1-4236-0280-3
 1. Canning and preserving. 2. Cookery, American—Southern style. I.
Title.
 TX603.D69 2008
 641.4—dc22
                      2008004274

To my grandmother, Weezie, a southern belle steeled by the Reconstruction and to my mother, Heywie, a debutante hardened by the Depression—two tough ladies who taught me all I needed to know before I was seven years old.

9   Acknowledgments

11   Introduction

15   PART ONE: CANNING

53   PART TWO: THE RECIPES

55   JANUARY
Lowcountry Pluff Mud

61   FEBRUARY
Pickled Garlic, Hot Pickled Garlic,
  or Fiery Pickled Garlic
Artichoke Pickles
Artichoke Relish
Artichoke Chow-Chow

71   MARCH
Strawberry Preserves
Pickled Asparagus

77   APRIL
Strawberry-Orange Marmalade
Pickled Beets

81   MAY
Uncle Patty's Garlic Pickles
Green Tomato Chow-Chow
Bread and Butter Pickles
Hot Chow-Chow
Green Tomato Pickle
Very Berry Preserves

91   JUNE
Green Tomato Relish
Green Tomato Chutney
Green Tomato Soup
Southern Tomato Sauce
Tomato Salsa
Gazpacho
Red Tomato Chutney
Tomato Ketchup
Red Tomato Relish
Pickled Shrimp
Seafood Cocktail Sauce
Charleston Creole Sauce
Charleston Gumbo
Dilled String Beans
Blackberry Preserves

contents

117 JULY
Peach Mint Preserves
Peach Preserves
Peach Salsa
Peach Chutney
Garden Vegetable Soup
Pepper Relish or Hot Pepper Relish
Fruit Chutney
Hot Pepper Jelly
Garlic Pepper Jelly
Blueberry Preserves
Blueberry Marmalade

135 AUGUST
Colonial Charleston Chutney
Whole Fig Preserves and Jam
Okra Pickles
There's Hot and Then There's
   Hot Sauce
Pickled Peaches
Peach Leather
Watermelon Rind Pickles

147 SEPTEMBER
Pear Chutney
Pear Relish
Ginger Pear Preserves
Corn Liquor BBQ Sauce

155 OCTOBER
Pumpkin Chips
Sweet Potato Butter

159 NOVEMBER
Cranberry Chutney
Mint Jelly

163 DECEMBER
Christmas Morning Marmalade
Christmas Pepper Jelly
Field Pea Relish

169 PART THREE: AFTERTHOUGHTS

172 RESOURCES

173 INDEX

acknowledgments

THE OCTOBER DAY when Christopher Robbins and Pete Wyrick approached me at the Charleston Farmers Market will be indelibly etched in my mind for all time. I was reluctant to take on this project, but the two have led me through a most exciting, new adventure. Both are wonderful men, and I cannot thank them enough for the final arm twist it took to do this book.

Had my son, Thomas, not taken the journey—not only by boat but by being my partner in our canning venture for all of those years when we struggled to make the business viable—we would never have had the products that we created. Working with one's father has got to be difficult, if not impossible, yet he stuck it out. His palate is flawless, and his understanding of what most people want is uncanny. This book is as much his as mine, for many of the recipes are ours.

After forty years without an English professor circling my punctuation errors and correcting my grammar in red pencil, I have found that I have much lacking in the field of the written word. Along came Cordon Bleu, Grand Diploma graduate and renowned, award-winning food writer Holly Herrick to the rescue. Her professional knowledge and ways guided me many times through the switchbacks of this culinary mountain road. When the recipes had been reduced for home use, she helped me test them, and it was she who added and subtracted ingredients to create the subtle nuances that make each recipe successful. More than that, she kept me smiling and going when I sometimes felt more like crying and quitting. Holly is a big part of this book.

A book is no different from the manufacture of a car or an airplane. The writer is the guy who gets his name on the book cover, but there are sixty or so other people of equal importance in the process. Each works as hard as the author, maybe harder and longer. To the entire family at Gibbs Smith, Publisher, the team of which I am a part, I thank you and I apologize if I made your tasks more difficult than they needed to be.

—Steve Dowdney

introduction

IT WAS THE FALL of '06 and I was busy. There was a crowd of locals and tourists encircling our booth at the Charleston Farmers Market, all vying for my attention. This Saturday ritual repeats itself weekly, until the rural fields surrounding the old city go fallow with winter's chill. Off to my right, two men beckoned. I held up my index finger, as if to say "I'll answer your question shortly." Busy making suggestions, taking money, and bagging products, I answered the usual hum of questions. The press of the crowd continued. Finally, the patient men's time came.

One asked. "Have you ever considered writing a book?"

I swallowed, and thought, *maybe good fortune isn't so elusive*. I returned to reality and chuckled, "Boy this is your lucky day; it was just this morning I put the finishing touches on my second novel."

The two men looked at each other and smiled. The taller one turned to me and spoke. "Sorry! Not that kind of book!"

"Do you make all these products?" the other inquired.

"Yes, sir," I answered. "I've been doing this for twelve years and I hope to keep doing it for another twelve. It's not the money, believe me, it's not the money. I do it for, for, well . . . ," I looked over my left shoulder. There she was, just the kind of person I had hoped to see.

"See that woman over yonder, the one getting ready to sample the artichoke relish?" I pointed to the far left corner of our space. "Watch!" I said. My eye told me she was a tourist; few locals carry a map of our town with the accompanying guide. She spread cream cheese on a cracker and then some relish. Two chews later her mouth stopped. Her eyes rolled. Before she could swallow, she was turning to her husband. She jabbed her index finger, pointing at the bowl while grunting. Finally, she was able to exclaim, "Oh, my God, you have got to try this!"

I returned to my conversation with the two men who would soon become my editor and my publisher. "That is why I do what I do. For me, canning gives a real feeling of accomplishment. There is little in my life that gives me more satisfaction than the scene you just witnessed, played over and over, with a diverse and growing array of products. Many I have created. Some of the recipes are as old as the Republic itself. I make them all."

"Back to our original question, would you be interested in writing a book on canning?"

canning

WHO

There are two "who's" to be addressed in this section. Who can do this thing called canning? And who is this author and what qualifications does he have?

The art of "putting up," as it is still called in the South, doesn't take a chef. It doesn't take a cook, it doesn't take any schooling, and there are as many guys as there are gals knocking out the jars. I often hear from curious customers when I offer them one of my recipes, "Are you kidding me? I'd burn water if I tried to boil it. I could never make that."

In fact, nothing more than the ability to read and follow a few simple steps are required to successfully produce the most wonderful preserves, condiments, soups and sauces you'll ever put in your mouth. Because of the added personal effort, many family dinners will become as exciting as dining in a fabulous restaurant. As an added bonus, you will feel that warm glow of satisfaction because of your "put up" additions—those little extras that made your dinner a unique, world-class event.

THE SECOND "WHO"

My careers have been diversified, to say the least. As was the law of the land at the time, after I graduated from college I became a soldier. Eventually, I found myself fighting, first in Africa and later in Vietnam. When peace came, I entered the world of real estate. Later, and still searching, I messed with boats on a professional level. Finally, I entered the heady arena of stocks and bonds. I became a vice president at a national investment house. My family lacked little, but still, nothing bought my fancy.

It took me fifty years before I found the meaningful satisfaction of canning. I was obviously a slow learner, since I was first exposed to the art when very young while living with my grandparents at Rockland Plantation in South Carolina. A war was raging, my father was overseas, and my mother worked for naval intelligence in a far away city. I was passed off to the loving care of my grandparents. What a pass-off—unconditional love on a southern plantation. Well, really it was only the remnants of a once great land grant, but still, by definition, it was a real plantation, a totally self-sufficient farm. We had cattle, pigs, chickens and fields of crops for both family and livestock. The farm was on an island and fronted on a river, so the bounty of the sea also graced the family table; crab, shrimp, mullet, flounder, bass, sea trout and a variety of small edible fish like croaker.

My grandfather fashioned a three-legged stool for me and, by age four, I could milk the cow. I watched him and learned to make butter, cottage cheese and ice cream. I knew how to pluck chickens, work fields and cut greens. While most kids are finicky about what goes into their mouths, I could spit out birdshot and keep right on eating quail without a second thought.

It was during this formative period that I also got my canning indoctrination. My grandmother not only put up for the Rockland pantry, she commercially produced a host of shelf-stable products, from pickled shrimp to Jerusalem artichokes, for many east coast stores. Her products became legendary. Even Clementine Paddleford, the renowned *New York Herald Tribune* food editor, once dedicated her column to her. The article was headlined, "Rockland Plantation Pickled Shrimp Invade Post-War New York." Little did I know then, those idyllic years, coupled with a wonderful grandmother and her commercial enterprise, would later meld into a most satisfying venture.

The restlessness and the searching that I presumed was part of life finally grabbed me by the throat. Events shook me to the core. It might have been that I was approaching fifty and somewhere deep inside a clock was telling me I didn't have forever to discover satisfaction. Who knows, it might have been something far simpler; then again, it might have been something so complex it's too spooky to contemplate. I often dwell on those times and events.

At any rate, to make a long story even longer, after steering so many clients into stocks, in the midst of the biggest bull market in history, I one day pushed back my chair and said, "That's it!" I walked out the office never to return.

After a period of decompression, my son and I boarded a tiny sailboat. We set to sea. We coped with calms and battled Pacific storms. After one fierce blow where we had struggled, cold and wet, through two days and nights to hold a course and keep afloat, we hove-to, exhausted. The wind had subsided. We slept. I dreamed. Across the ages came a grandmother's call. "Go to Charleston, pickle shrimp!" Ten thousand miles later our prow slid into the famous pluff mud of the Lowcountry. I was home.

Father and son were now ready to answer grandmother's call. We set to work. By year ten we had become the talk of the town when it came to locally produced jams, condiments, soups and sauces. We were turning out over sixty products packaged under a variety of labels. Each day fifteen hundred jars, cans and bags would leave our facility. Some we sold at local farmers markets, some we shipped to distant admirers. Many were destined for the shelves of local purveyors. Numerous articles, local, regional and national appeared in newspapers and magazines. Similar stories were broadcast over radio and television. Friends from as far away as California and Hawaii would call to say they had seen us on television.

These cercis were never our intent. All we set out to do was to create a wonderful product for our local economy. We wanted the very best, a product just like my grandmother made, just like all grandmothers once made when life was simple.

Fourteen years have passed. Our involvement has changed. We no longer put in fifteen-hour days seven days a week. A younger crew bought those reins. Mine, now, is an advisory role, and yet, I remain

Artichoke Relish
2/10/07

Artichoke Relish
2/10/07

Garlic Pickle
2/12/07

fully committed. I search out and create new and exciting recipes and I continue to enjoy selling our products at local markets. Through those tumultuous years, son Tom and I remained best friends. We can laugh now as we recall some crisis situation of the past. In a greater sense, it is as if that call to can from across the ages paved a highway on which we both now travel.

WHY

"Canning," the idiomatic gerund for preserving produce and pre-pared recipes in special vessels, is a misnomer. It is rare that a home kitchen will use an actual can. Metal closures are nearly impossible to come by in small quantities (that is to say, in lots of less than twenty-five thousand) and cans require expensive and complex sealing machinery. Consequently, special "canning" jars are used, and have been since 1810, long before metal cans were perfected. In the early days of the twentieth century, when our country still clung to its agrarian roots and later when the Depression tightened the nation's purse strings, industrious family members processed and put up all they could of the fresh bounty locally available. The effort saved money and insured a well-stocked larder, regardless of a family's economic plight.

Our world has changed. Commercially available produce is now gathered and shipped from many different countries. What is winter here is summer in Peru. Modern high-speed transportation, flash freezing, nitrogen gas protection, chilled shipping containers, and a host of other protective sciences ensure that perishable products are delivered to grocery stores with a degree of freshness year-round.

To preserve, most plain vegetables require the application of very high heat, temperatures in excess of the boiling point of water. This can only be achieved in a "retort," the commercial term for a pressure canning vessel or pressure cooker. A home-canned vegetable is not fresher or better than a store bought fresh one, even one that has traveled thousand of miles over several weeks.

Pressure canning is complex. It is beyond the scope of this book and might best be left in the past, at least for the home processor. But if one concentrates his energy on special products like the ones in this book (preserves, relishes, chutneys, soups, sauces and pickles), the results, even for the amateur on his or her first attempt, will be better than anything one can purchase anywhere.

This book will guide you step-by-step through the preparation of products that will convert a boring family repast into an exciting dinner time adventure. You will put up goodies that you'll use as hors d'oeuvres when entertaining. Friends will ask, "Where in the world did you find this?" Your proud response will be, "I made it!" You'll put up preserves that, as gifts, will become the rage among friends. Some recipes you'll make don't exist on store shelves because of labor and produce requirements. Everything that you produce will be far better than what is available for purchase.

There is a reason for this. The quality of commercial products has continued to escalate. However, when using the word "quality," I am referring to the fancy glass packaging, eye-catching labels, and those special additives put in to maintain color and "freshness." All this might appear to be fine, but the actual taste of products we purchase has not improved. In fact, as the complexities of industrialization and competition have increased, the taste factor, in many cases, has eroded. The pretty jar and fancy label do not matter to our palate.

Why such craziness? A manufacturer receives only a small fraction of what one will pay for a jar. There are transportation costs and there are distributors and stores, all demanding their share of the profit. Worse, once on the store shelf, a jar must compete for a customer's dollar and there are many brands vying for purchase.

There are four ways a manufacturer can compete: advertising, price, label and container. Notice, taste is not in the competitive mix. It is unfortunate, but economics sometimes brings out the worst in business. Items manufactured competitively by the lowest bidder might work in the airplane business, but they crash in the food producing business. Ingredient availability is a key culprit. Produce needs to be brought from fields, gathered and sorted at central distribution points, shipped to far away local distribution centers, allocated, delivered, cleaned and prepared. Before processing takes place, maybe a week has passed, maybe a month, maybe longer. From the beginning, the best of a lot, the most expensive, has gone to restaurants and retailers.

Consider for a moment the simple strawberry. When one ventures into a field to select a berry, so ready for picking that it falls off the plant, it is full of flavor and aroma. It's a luscious, unbelievable creation. At those times, I wish that the spring of the year be eternal. For each dozen picked, at least one cannot help but fall into my mouth. This spectacular fruit has been created by good growing conditions: the right soil, hot sun and little rain as the berries ripen. Two days after picking, regardless of how the fruit is stored, spots will develop. By the next day the condition has worsened and by the fourth day one has no choice but to discard the remains.

How then do prominent national companies make strawberry preserves? Most have two choices, use frozen fruit or use berries picked green and artificially ripened while they journey toward jam. Neither berry will ever compete with ripe-picked fruit, nor will the preserves they make. When a family makes their own, it is much like original art as compared to a print. A similar story can be told with every commercial ingredient. This is why home canned is far superior!

Our lives have become filled. We find ourselves too busy. There is too much to squeeze into the hours. So slowly, over the past four decades, Americans have begun to purchase many once time-consuming homemade items, trading dollars for more time. Manufacturers know that today we are willing to consume food products that our forefathers would not consider edible. They know that we are willing to settle for less in the name of convenience.

Here's a tale of what I mean. When I was a parent of pre-teenage boys, one Sunday morning I arose early to get a head start on breakfast for the gang. I squeezed many pounds of the sweetest, just-picked oranges a friend brought me from Florida. I placed the glasses of juice in the freezer to chill while I continued with the morning preparations. During the kids' breakfast, I had a food epiphany. The children sat around the dining room table chatting with each other as I served them. The first to try the juice looked startled. I had anticipated surprise. I had waited in the dining room to catch the expressions. In the Northwest, ripe-picked Florida oranges are an unheard of anomaly.

"What is this?" The young taster asked.

I explained. The others tasted, getting puzzled looks on their faces. They looked at one another. My two boys looked at me, embarrassed, like I was the nut case they always knew I was. Finally, there was a consensus at the table; it didn't taste like orange juice, no orange juice they'd ever tasted. Then one of the boys delivered the blow that got me thinking. "Did I have any regular orange juice, like the real stuff you mix with water?" he asked. That was how conditioned a rising generation was becoming to a sub-standard quality.

Here's another example. Each June, the best of the best commercial gourmet kitchens gather at the Fancy Food Show at the Javits Center in New York City. They come together to present their goods to the great store buyers from all over the country. "Tasting is not what this is about," a veteran Fancy Food Show colleague told me. "What's important is how the product shows and its profit margin," he added. How far we have distanced ourselves from grandmothers' kitchens! This book was put together to take you back.

There is more than just taste when one puts up. One might continue for the sake of art. As humans we crave to create. It is one of those traits that separate us from other earthlings. A Doubting Thomas might say, "But you are not creating; you are using a recipe." Yes, we are, but it is still art and canning is still art. It is no different from the artist with easel and palate sitting on the beach looking seaward. The artist didn't create the sea or the scene, yet that's his recipe. He paints it. Putting up will provide our table and our family and friends with a diverse array of products, not generally available on the markets, products that are made with just picked, wonderfully tasting ingredients. Finally, and important to our culture, we are keeping alive an art of our past while recreating a standard against which commercial producers can and will be judged.

Food is king. On a national level during the last score of years, food and cooking has grown from necessity into a kind of mainstream mania. There are television shows on cooking. Small towns now have gourmet restaurants. Supermarkets have special gourmet and organic produce sections. Culinary stores sell equipment and cookbooks, and cooking classes are being taught all across the country. A revolution has begun. And yet there are few books that specialize in putting up food as we once did in kitchens across America. Most of those in print are nondiscriminatory, featuring everything that is able to be put up. This book addresses only those products that can be made better by you in your home.

WHERE

Just about every kitchen has ample capacity to become a home canning center. Federal law requires that products produced for consumption by the public be made in an inspected and approved facility used only for the commercial enterprise. In other words, if you intend to sell what you make, plan on using something other than your home kitchen. But for home use and gift giving, your own kitchen will work just fine.

Regardless of its size, with planning and organization, your existing kitchen will do. The commercial kitchen where my son and I produced those thousands of jars each day exceeded 7,500 square feet, but the kitchen where I now put up my products for home use, where I create new recipes and make my hand-crafted gifts, is tiny, just 6 x 7 feet or 42-square feet. I have two small counters, neither one a yard long, a four-burner stove, a single sink, and a refrigerator. The kitchen is about as plain vanilla, a single scoop at that, as one can get and yet I have everything I need. There is some specialized equipment that I use and that you will need. Many of the items you might already have, but others you will have to purchase—which brings us to the next section.

WHAT

As with any new endeavor, one's going to need some special items. Much of what is needed for canning might already be in your kitchen. Some is unique to canning and will need to be purchased. Don't fret. The good news is that nothing required is expensive. In the following pages are two lists. The first is essential; the second makes the canning process quicker and easier.

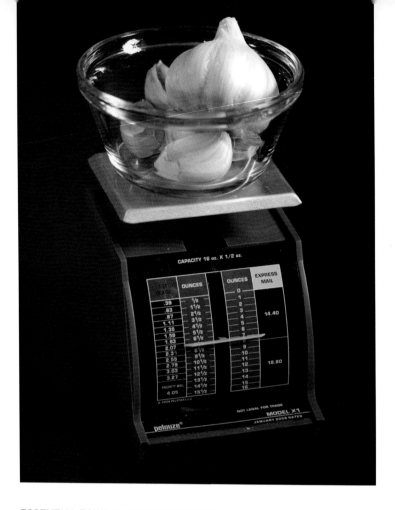

ESSENTIAL EQUIPMENT AND SUPPLIES

- **Weighing scale 0 to 1 pound:** I use a postal scale. These can be purchased at stores like Office Depot and Staples. Food scales are more expensive and are available in culinary stores, online and at restaurant supply stores. A postal scale will work just fine.

- **Weighing scale 1 to 10 pounds:** The same stores carry these scales. Just one word of caution: I have listed two separate scales because light weights on inexpensive scales made to measure heavier loads do not record accurately.

- **Canning funnels:** This funnel is canning specific. It is designed to fit firmly into the mouth of the specialized canning jar. The throat of the funnel extends down into the jar exactly to the canning line. When one fills to the bottom of the funnel they have fully filled a jar. These funnels can be purchased at stores like Wal-Mart, ordered from stores like Kitchen Craft or found at numerous websites online.

- **Spatulas:** The newer silicon spatulas are wonderful. Unlike their rubber ancestors, they do not deteriorate and leave behind bits of material in the chutney. I also use a large commercial metal

spatula, the kind a line cook would use to flip burgers on a grill. The blade is long and wide, 3 x 7 inches and has a blunt, squared end. This is one of my favorite tools. I find it an invaluable asset. When stirring a pot, I make circular sweeps, mixing all that is on or near the edges, and then zigzag across the pot bottom. The hard, straight edges move all that is in contact with the hot sides and bottom so nothing burns. Unlike a flexible spatula, the metal will not go over a lump stuck on the bottom. Proper use of this tool, along with diligent stirring, ensures nothing is in contact with the high heat long enough to affect the taste of the finished product. The spatula is commercial and carried by restaurant supply stores or can be found online.

- **Measuring spoons and cups:** These are probably already in your kitchen, but if not, they are readily available almost anywhere. One will need a measuring range from 1/4 teaspoon up to 4 cups. For the cups, don't use glass. If glass breaks there is always a

chance an errant shard might find its way into your ingredients. Smaller measures come in plastic and stainless. Two- and four-cup measures are mostly in clear plastic. The problem with most plastic measures is they have the increments painted on the outside. The markings wear off quickly. Try to find measurers with raised markings. They'll last many seasons.

- **Sharp knives:** Okay, I'm a guy and knives are a guy thing. Regardless, knives are an essential tool in the canning process. In case you haven't already noticed, I'm an old-fashioned type, so I like carbon steel blades. I maintain them with steel and stone to shaving-edge specifications. Still, on occasion, I find myself reaching into the cutlery drawer to get a serrated blade. Of course, I'm embarrassed and immediately after use wash and return it lest I get confronted about my extravagant Sabatier knife expenditures.

  All kitchens are stocked with knives, but sharp knives make processing work much easier and more professional. The blades one will use the most are a paring knife and a heavy-duty 8-inch chef's knife. Get a quality knife sharpener, either stone or steel, and use it frequently.

- **Cutting boards:** One large one will work. Having two, one very small, will help with counter management if space is limited. I use bamboo. The soft wood protects the edges of my wonderful blades and the renewable, farmed resource, protects our remaining hardwood forests.

- **Cooking pots:** This is worth a winded discussion. Not any pot will do! When preparing recipes for canning, as you will learn in the How section, all mixtures are acid-based. Acids react with aluminum and uncoated iron and your finished product will be tainted. It's also possible it will discolor and might possess a metallic flavor. Neither condition is acceptable. Further, the negative effects of ingesting aluminum are still being researched. This leaves copper, enameled steel or iron, and stainless steel.

  Our foremothers knew what they were doing in the kitchen when they cooked with copper. Copper pots are wonderful cookers

because they are excellent conductors of heat. Kept polished, they are beautiful and add a nice touch to the look of any kitchen. The inside of a copper pot must be coated to prevent a lethal poison, cuprous oxide, from entering cooked food products.

In times past, copper pots were coated in tin. Some still are. When the tin wears off, the pot must be taken to a tinker, a person knowledgeable in the art of pot repair, for a new lining. I haven't met any tinkers in recent years and I probably won't any time soon. More recently, because of advances in metallurgy technology, some copper pots are coated with stainless steel. Now we are talking really big bucks. I suggest you read on without making a purchase quite yet.

Enameled pots, pressed from light-gauge steel, are a waste of money. They do not last and they do not conduct heat well. Enameled pots made from heavy cast iron conduct and distribute heat very well, but any pot that is enameled or ceramic coated, light or heavy, only lasts until it receives the first inside ding. Shortly thereafter, it begins to rust. My advice is, don't bother.

Stainless steel, even heavy stainless, is not a good conductor of heat. The spots where the burner is concentrated will get very hot while the rest of the pot remains relatively cool. This means constant stirring. It is just a matter of time before something burns.

When a product becomes scorched, the burnt taste will get canned right along with the ingredients. Modern cookware features healthy, low-maintenance stainless inside and out with a sandwich of multiple, good heat-conducting metals like copper and aluminum. More expensive varieties have the multiple layers going all the way up or part way up the sides. On less expensive models, the sandwich is limited to the bottom. It's your call. I use pots I found at Wal-Mart. In my opinion, they deliver by far the most bang for the buck. I have a 12-quart and a 22-quart pot.

- **Water bath pot with rack:** This is a totally specialized piece of equipment but is not one that is going to break a bank. Most of the systems available are comprised of a light, enameled steel pot with a galvanized rack that holds seven jars. This will do just fine. I

use two of these so I can prepare a baker's dozen jars plus at once. Over time, the cheap enameled pots will be replaced with more substantial vessels that transfer heat faster, but there is no rush.

- **Adjustable cook's thermometer:** These are available hanging on grocery shelves. It is the kind that looks like a ballpoint pen with a dial on top, the type one sticks in and removes. It is not the kind that is left stuck in meat in the oven. I have purchased thermometers in restaurant supply stores, grocery stores and at Wal-Mart, of course. I keep several on hand. One is as good as another as long as it can be adjusted. To tell if the meter can be calibrated, look on the back side of the face. If there is a hex headed protuberance, it is adjustable. Its plastic sheath is usually the adjusting tool. Test and adjust once a month.

- **Colanders:** These handy items are probably already in your kitchen inventory, but if not, purchase the biggest one you can comfortably store. Nothing fancy; plastic is fine.

- **Canning jars and lids:** You will need 8-, 16- and 32-ounce regular, as opposed to wide mouth, jars. Like the funnel and water bath equipment, this product is canning specific. Canning jar glass is thicker and more durable than regular jar glass and can take rapid changes in temperature without shattering; the threaded top section is of special material and engineered so the lids, which have an applied ring of a rubber-like coating, will create an easy and excellent seal on the finished product. During the seasons of harvest, twelve-jar cases with lids are available in many stores including your favorite supermarket. If you have a Big Lots nearby, try them. They have better prices than what small companies pay for these jars wholesale, direct from the same manufacturer, and they inventory many pallets of all the common sizes during the harvest seasons. If you can store them, stock up! Your next best price might be Wal-Mart—where else!

- **Chemicals needed for canning:**

    Sodium hypoclorite: A jug of regular grocery store bleach like Clorox meets this requirement. You will dilute this chemical and use it to sterilize jars and wipe down counters for bacteria-free canning.

    Sodium chloride: This is the chemical name for salt. It is in this section because not just any salt will work. One cannot use salt with iodine or any additives including anti-caking agents. Sea salt is not an option either. At many grocery stores one can purchase 25-pound bags of pure evaporated sodium chloride produced by Morton. The cost is about four dollars. Canning salt, the same item but in the canning section of stores costs ten times this amount or more! The issue is that the salt must be pure.

    Distilled water: Not a chemical. It is, in fact, the exact opposite; it's chemical free. It can be purchased almost anywhere and is very different from regular water. For some testing one should use only distilled water. A gallon jug will last a long time.

    Citric Acid: This is used to increase the acidity of certain canned products. It is found wherever canning supplies are sold.

    Canning or slacked lime: This is a food-grade lime that, when mixed with water, will maintain crispness in certain vegetables.

    Alum: This is another keep-it-crisp chemical. It can be purchased at most drug stores but might have to be ordered, so plan a few days ahead.

Short-range pH paper: Don't let this intimidate you! It might sound impressive, but these rolls or test strips are simply acid-sensitive papers like the litmus paper one might have used in a high school or college chemistry or science class. You will need to get short-range paper. Rolls come with a range between 3.4 and 4.8, strips between 3.0 and 5.0. Rolls are better for our purpose. They are less expensive and have a more narrow range. In my grandmother's day, when she put up foods, she followed time honored recipes and hoped. Because the acid levels of various fruits and vegetables fluctuate with ripeness and variety, this testing will insure the complete safety of your finished product, something our forebearers didn't do. Phew, we made it! To purchase pH paper, check the Resources section on page 173.

NICE EQUIPMENT TO HAVE

- **Blender:** For puréeing, nothing beats this piece of equipment. Although used infrequently, when needed, it will save in time its inconsequential cost. Also, for pH testing a finished product, it makes for quick sessions.
- **Food processor:** At one time this piece of equipment was for the rich and famous. A few makes still are. Some units last while others barely make it through a season. Two years ago I bought a bigger, just slightly more expensive unit with a direct drive. I have been thrilled with the performance and the bigger bowl is just an added benefit. The machine turns many laborious chores into the turn of the dial.
- **Large measuring pitchers:** These handy measurers can really speed up a process. One can always use four 4-cup measures to accomplish a gallon measurement, but with a single half-gallon or gallon pitcher it takes less time and there is less chance for error. I cannot tell you the number of times I have counted out three or four measures when the phone rang. Let's see, now where was I?
- **Heat proof gloves:** I have never used a pair, but once or twice I wish I had. Jams, for example, must be brought to a strong boil while stirring. Unlike more watery products that boil at 212 degrees and have little density, which means they cool fast, even on skin,

preserves are thick and are upwards of 220 degrees. This is closer to napalm. When a boil bubble splatters on your wrist or arm you know it. During fruit season my right hand and lower arm look like I have a case of "right-arm measles."

- **pH meter:** This is getting high tech, but I added it for those who want extreme accuracy. You will learn more about acidity and canning shortly. The FDA requires a commercial packer to use a pH meter to measure acid levels on any product canned above pH 4.00. This is a bit extreme. Above 4.2 might be a more realistic limit, but it's not their nickel so what do they care? The price range for meters is from fifty dollars upward. If you do get a meter, you will also need calibration buffer solutions. The maximum pH for any recipe in this book is 4.2 and pH paper will work fine. If you decide to create a recipe, then you are on your own.

HOW

Canning is not rocket science. Thus far you have encountered terms like acidity, pH, conductivity and density, but these are only the jargon of the trade. Canning is as easy as boiling water, but it's more fun and far more rewarding.

I have read many books on the subject of canning. I have yet to read a book that sets forth the procedures as required by the Food and Drug Administration (FDA) for safely canning acid and acidified foods for commercial application. The FDA's mission is to insure the safety of the people. President Reagan once jested that the most terrifying words one could hear in America are "I am from the government and I'm here to help." Sadly, in most instances those words ring truer than truth itself. However, the FDA, in insuring safe canning practices, has in fact simplified a process that basically remained unchanged since before the turn of the twentieth century. A miracle by government is truly a miracle!

The canning steps outlined in this manual are the same as required by the FDA. They are exactly the same methods and procedures every commercial packer must follow. The steps provide the safest, most accurate method of canning, and will insure a good, sealed product that will be of the very highest quality.

HOT PACKING

When the product has cooked the suggested amount of time, check the pH with a tear of pH paper. If within the guidelines given for the recipe, continue; if not, follow the recipe instructions for increasing acidity. Next, check the temperature of the product. It must be, at least, at the minimum temperature stated in the recipe.

With the testing done, you are ready to proceed. I use two measuring cups for the filling process. I use one to scoop the product from the pot into a second, bigger measure. I then hang the first cup on the inside pot edge. This way I do not have a dripping cup making a mess of my canning area. With the canning funnel in the mouth of the sterilized jar, pour in the mixture until it, at least, touches the bottom of the funnel. It is important, also, not to fill a jar too full or in other ways contaminate the sealing edge—the very top edge of the jar—during this process. An edge can also get contaminated from product on the outside of the funnel's throat. In time you'll have several funnels, keeping the extras rinsing in a bowl of water.

In the meantime, wipe the lower exterior of the funnel clean periodically with the cloth treated with the sterile solution. If the sealing edge of a jar does get contaminated, carefully wipe it clean with the same sterile dishcloth. Clean edges insure good seals! Once the pitcher is empty, maybe after filling two or three jars, prepare to seal the full jars. Caution: they will be hot. Place lids on jars, making sure none are cross threaded, and tighten. Once sealed, turn each jar upside down for a minimum of 2 minutes. Longer is fine, but not long enough for products like preserves to jell. This inversion accomplishes several tasks. The hot solution softens the rubbery substance on the lids to guarantee a good seal, and the heat further sterilizes the lid and the neck of the jar. Continue these processes until the pot is empty. If a last jar only partially fills, cap it and place in the refrigerator for final testing and near term use. Turn the jars upright any time after the specified 2-minute period and wipe clean.

WATER BATHING

Follow the recipe instructions for packing the sterilized jars with ingredients. The rack that comes with a water bath pot holds seven

pint or half-pint jars. Place the seven or first seven in the rack. Prepare the liquid, as described in the recipe, on the stove and fill each jar to the canning line (the ring just below the threads), starting with the center jar. This center jar will be designated the cold jar because it was filled first and therefore will be the coolest.

Next, screw on the lids, just barely finger tight, on all but the center jar. On the center jar, screw on a lid with a small hole in the middle that you have made so you can insert a thermometer. Insert the thermometer, making sure the tip reaches to the bottom. Next, lower the jars into the boiling water that you have previously adjusted so the level reaches only to the canning line, the ring just below the threading. As the jars go in, the water will stop boiling. As soon as it begins to boil again, turn down the heat, a little at a time, so there is never a rapid boil. Rapid boiling could cause water to seep into the jars. When the specified temperature is attained, wait 2 minutes and remove the rack. Tighten the lids on each jar, being very careful; these jars are very hot! Lastly, replace the thermometer lid with a standard lid and tighten. After each lid is tightened, turn the jar upside down for a minimum of 2 minutes.

With both methods of canning, vacuum, sterilization, temperature and acidity combine to create a safe, shelf-stable product.

VACUUM
This is created by the hot material inside the jar shrinking as it cools and is why a positive seal between lid and jar is so important. It is also why you must fill each jar to the canning line just below the threaded section. Lesser amounts of product will create more space and reduce the amount of vacuum; a bad seal will also prevent a vacuum from being formed. Some canning lids have a "button" in the center of the lid; when sucked down, it indicates a good vacuum. Some lids don't have buttons. I tap each lid with a teaspoon after the jar has cooled. The sound of an unsealed jar rings hollow and is very different from the sound of a sealed one. With both types of lids, as the jars cool you will hear them click as the vacuum increases. Jars that don't seal are fine if kept in the refrigerator.

STERILIZATION

Clean jars and lids are important in preventing the growth of mold. This is why we first wash and then use chemicals to sterilize the jars and lids. To save time in future canning, a suggestion might be to measure the amount of water necessary to fill your sink to a workable level and then mark the level on the sink with an awl. If you don't want to scratch the sink, or if it is porcelain, with a ruler measure the depth of the required amount of water, or make a gauge, like with a marked stick. Then, each time you are ready to sterilize jars, you need only to run warm water to the correct level before stirring in the appropriate measure of bleach (2 tablespoons per gallon of water).

TEMPERATURE

Pathogens, the bacteria and molds we don't want to grow in our finished product, are destroyed at varying temperatures based upon the acidity level. Below is a chart of canning temperatures for various acid levels. The correct canning temperature for each recipe in this book is detailed in the recipe. However, if you begin creating recipes of your own, this chart will be necessary. It is

also important to remember that these temperatures are the initial temperature of the product after it has been introduced into the jar. As a rule of thumb, add 5 degrees to compensate for a room temperature jar.

MAXIMUM PH	MINIMUM DEGREES F
3.9 and lower	182 degrees F
4.1	185 degrees F
4.2	190 degrees F
4.3	195 degrees F
4.4	205 degrees F
4.5	210 degrees F

To make sure your thermometer is correctly calibrated, fill a small saucepan three-fourths full of water (distilled water gives a more accurate reading, but is not necessary). When the water has reached a rolling boil, lower in the thermometer, tip first, until the probe is at least halfway submerged. Read the meter. It should read exactly 212 degrees F if you live at sea level. If you live at sea level and it does not, adjust to 212 degrees following the manufacturer's instructions. For kitchens above sea level see chart below.

ALTITUDE TEMPERATURE AT WHICH WATER BOILS

Sea level	212 degrees F
1000 feet	210 degrees F
2000 feet	208 degrees F
3000 feet	206 degrees F
4000 feet	205 degrees F
5000 feet	203 degrees F
6000 feet	201 degrees F

This table is rounded down to the next whole number. For folks who live at high altitudes, some of the recipes call for canning temperatures that may exceed the boiling point of water at your altitude. Don't despair. Sugar, salt and nearly everything in a recipe increases a liquid's boiling point.

ACIDITY

I saved the best for last! During the first Gulf War, I remember seeing a political cartoon of an Iraqi scud missile with a jar of string beans lashed to the warhead. The cartoonist must have put up a jar or two in his day, for those of us involved in canning are most cognizant of *clostridium botulinum*, a bacteria found everywhere on earth. Actually it is in common, everyday dirt, but remains harmless until it is subjected to an anaerobic environment, a place without oxygen. It is then that the bacteria will grow, releasing spores of a deadly neurotoxin called botulism. In terrorist jargon, that's a nerve agent and thus came the inspiration for the cartoon. When I was going through Green Beret training at the JFK Center for Special Warfare, during the demolition phase we learned how to mix fertilizer with diesel fuel to make an expedient explosive. After the Oklahoma bombing catastrophe, nitrogen fertilizer became a controlled substance. I often wonder if the string bean will be next?

When we create a vacuum in a jar to prevent yeasts and molds from growing, we also create that same potentially dangerous anaerobic environment; however, because the acidity of the product inhibits the spore forming *clostridium botulinum,* preventing harmful growth, this is not a problem, and there is never a concern as long as a product's acidity is and remains below pH 4.6. For acidified recipes, both water bath and hot pack, one must maintain an acid level below 4.6. It is for this reason we always check the acidity of an acidified recipe both before and 24 hours after we can it.

To reduce any confusion about acid levels, the lower the pH number the more acidic is the product. The higher the number the more alkaline or base, the product. The pH scale goes from 0–14, with seven being neutral and the division between acidic and alkaline, and acid level pH 4.6 being the safety cut off for water bath and hot pack canning.

0	4.6	7	14
MOST ACID		NEUTRAL	MOST ALKALINE

How one achieves the necessary acid environment when preparing recipes is by natural induction, artificial additives or a combination of both. Every living organism has a natural pH range. Actually, one of the distinguishing features between a fruit and a vegetable is its acidity. Above pH 4.7 a plant is no longer a fruit. The fruit with the highest pH is the tomato. Yes, a tomato is a fruit; it is a berry with a typical pH range between 4.1 and 4.6.

A complex acidified recipe might contain multiple ingredients with pH ranges from 2.5 all the way up to 11.0, like okra, for example. Initially, when a recipe is developed, the acid level is measured. If the mixture does not have a wide margin of safety, acids are introduced to make it a safe canning candidate. This is most often accomplished by the addition of citric acid, lemon juice, vinegar or a combination.

ACIDIFIED CANNING

Each recipe in this book has been pH tested. Each has a wide margin of safety, with no recipe exceeding a pH higher than 4.2 when properly prepared using the correct ingredients. Further, each recipe is designated either acid, sugar saturated, or acidified; and, if acidified, what pH range to expect. Just the same, if the person in the kitchen happens to forget an ingredient, the acidity of the final product could be dangerously altered. This is why we do an initial test before canning. It would be a shame to have to redo or throw out one's work for the sake of a 5-second test. As a finished product cools, sometimes the pH rises ever so slightly because there is a temperature to pH relationship. More pronounced could be the balance that continues for several hours while penetrating acids mix with alkaline solids. In theory, these might make a difference. In reality, they do not seem to, but it is good, safe canning practice to test again after 24 hours to make sure the pH is below the 4.6 level.

The acidification method most often used is the addition of vinegar. There are many types and several common percentages of this acid. When canning we use only 5 percent. A lower percentage might cause a dangerously high pH. See "Types of Canning" on page 59 for more information on the different types of canning.

PH TESTING

The initial test for hot pack recipes is simple. Stir the product in the pot and dip in a small tear of pH paper. Compare the color on the strip to the code on the pH paper pack. My workers had a saying, "Green is clean," meaning acid level is sufficient. You'll understand better after you make your first test. With a water bath recipe, before the jar lid holding the thermometer is applied, scoop $1/2$ teaspoon of liquid from the jar and test with pH paper. This test is accomplished to make sure the liquid used for acidification is in fact strong enough to do the job. If not, it is because the mixture has been prepared incorrectly or the acidity of the vinegar is less than 5 percent. Final testing of water bath recipes are the important tests.

Testing after twenty-four hours takes a little more time. For well-blended, hot pack recipes, like chutneys and relishes, place a small amount—about a tablespoonful—into a clean bowl or a blender. Add about a cup of distilled water and mix well, cutting up, crushing or blending the solids. Test with the pH paper to insure the completed product remains safe. Canning jars come in several sizes, the smallest being 4 ounces. I have a case of these I use just for testing. When hot packing, I fill a 4-ounce test jar and turn it upside down just like any other jar. When water bathing, I put in all the required ingredients of the regular canning jar but in a quantity commensurate with the size of the regular canning jar. For example, if canning pints, I put in one-fourth of the amount. I fill the little jar with the hot liquid and put on the lid. I do not water bath this jar. I put it in the refrigerator and test it the following day and then discard. To test a water bath or hot pack product with quantities of big, solid pieces, remove a piece of each primary ingredient, rinse with distilled water, place in a blender or bowl with about a cup of distilled water. Blend or crush well and then test pH. Any number below 4.6 means the product is safe.

VACUUM TESTING

One test is performed on all jars: a vacuum test. This checks the jar lids for a proper seal. The test can be performed any time after the jar has cooled. Use a teaspoon and tap the lid right on its center. An unsealed jar will sound different. Take an empty jar, fill it with water, put a lid on it and tap. This is the sound you don't want to hear.

CANNING ACID PRODUCTS

Some putting up can be done without pH testing because of the natural acid levels present in the ingredients or because with the amount of sugar used there is no water content. Preserves, jams and jellies are three of these. All the other safe measures—temperature, sterilization and vacuum—must be taken to insure top-quality canning and award-winning products.

TRICKS OF THE TRADE

Like in any new adventure there are some things that pros know and do that make the job easier. Here are a few we learned, most of them the hard way.

Liquids: Liquids tend to make a recipe runny. Often cooking times include the time necessary to eliminate excess liquid. Unfortunately, long cook times often cook the fresh-just-preserved-taste right out of the product. This is why on some recipes it says to squeeze the tomatoes. Also, when a recipe says to drain, drain well, very well—the less liquid the better.

Dicing/chopping: This is often simply a matter of presentation in many cases. For example, a tiny bell pepper square looks much better in pepper jelly than does a ragged chunk, but there is more. When using a food processor, the blade will often beat the ingredient into a runny mush. If it is only flavor that we seek, this is okay, but if it is the individual taste of the single ingredient, it becomes a problem. Add a little water to the food processor before pulsing and drain well after completion. This will help.

Preparing bell peppers: Chefs make an elaborate ritual over peppers, cutting them into strips, then slicing the veins off, dusting off the seeds and then dicing the strips. Our way is faster and, for your purposes, equally effective. Cut the pepper in half lengthwise. Rip out, by hand, the seed-stem clusters in both halves. Shake any additional seeds away. It doesn't hurt to leave a few. Slice each half in half again, lengthwise. The pepper is now ready to be worked and you have spent fifteen seconds.

Hot peppers: Wear gloves! Not only can peppers burn your hands and keep burning for many hours, your hands will continue to transfer the heat to everything you touch. Rub your eye, go to the bathroom—get the picture? The flavor in a pepper is in the skin, while most of the heat is in the veins and the seeds. One can tweak heat by removing some or all of the latter two. The fastest method

of seeding and veining is to cut the stem end off the pepper, slice the pepper lengthwise and run a gloved thumbnail or a teaspoon to scrape out the seeds and veins. If by chance one's hands do begin to burn, washing them in whole milk will help.

Making preserves: An old lady came up to my farmers market booth, picked up a jar of strawberry preserves, turned it on its side and rolled the jar in her hand. She looked at me, amazed. "This could win a blue ribbon at the Oklahoma State Fair," she exclaimed. I didn't know what she was talking about, but I learned. Once pectin begins forming the jelling chains, its getting time to can. This does not take a specified amount of time, like the books say, because fruit has differing amounts of liquids, depending on growing conditions. The rolling boil cooks off the excess water, but if there is little to begin with, it takes less time and if there is more it takes more time. This is why it is prudent to test for jelling with the stirrer. I allow the preserves to run off the tip of my metal spatula. If it runs like water, more boiling is needed. But when it makes long teardrop drips, it is getting ready. Go 30 seconds to 1 minute more. Why all

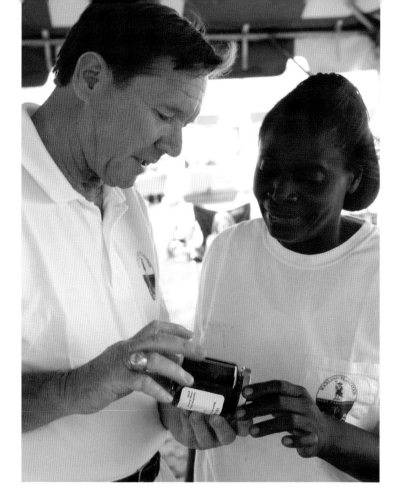

the fuss? Preserves and jams can get tough and rubbery if cooked too long. This woman was actually checking to see if my preserves fell away from the edge of the jar; as she rolled the jar, the break followed all around. She tasted and was impressed a second time. Still, she didn't buy the jar.

Bay leaves: These and other herbs and spices that will later be removed are usually tied in a cheesecloth bag for the cooking period. You will be doing a lot of stirring, and once a bag breaks open and you have to fish out each leaf and clove, you will seek a better solution. My son did just that. We began putting the to-be-removed-ingredients in a saucepan with a little boiling water. After boiling for 15 minutes, adding water if necessary, with strainer in one hand, we'd pour the flavored liquid into the recipe and discard the depleted herbs.

Getting smells off one's hands: If a good washing doesn't do the trick—and most of the time it won't—try rubbing your hands on anything stainless steel: a spoon, pot, whatever; this really helps.

GLOSSARY OF PREPARATION TERMS, MEASUREMENTS & ABBREVIATIONS

There are some technical words used to describe the way ingredients should be prepared and processed. These definitions will help by providing a standard in preparation.

Blanch: To pour boiling water over or submerge into boiling water for a time specified.

Boil: A boil where bubbles continuously form.

Chop: Cut larger than minced, like diced, but with no specific shape.

Cook: To hold at a specified temperature or just below boil for a specified period.

Dice: Cut into small squares (about $1/4$ inch).

Dice large: Cut into bigger squares ($3/8$ to $1/2$ inch).

Heat: To bring to specified temperature.

Low boil: A boil where periodic bubbles form.

Mince: Cut or chopped into tiny little pieces.

Purée: To blend in a blender until smooth and without lumps.

Rolling boil: A boil where the surface is fully involved.

Simmer: To heat for a period of time at a low temperature.

SMALL MEASUREMENTS USED IN A KITCHEN

This section is included because you might want to make more or less of a specific recipe. Recipes that can be doubled or halved are indicated with each recipe.

Dry Measure

1 teaspoon = a basic measure

1 tablespoon = 3 teaspoons

16 tablespoons = 1 cup

Liquid Measure

1 fluid ounce = a basic measure

8 fluid ounces = 1 cup

2 cups = 1 pint

2 pints = 1 quart

4 quarts = 1 gallon

Avoirdupois Measure

1 ounce = a basic measure

16 ounces = 1 pound

There is the old saying, "A pint's a pound the world around." This is true only for pure water, yet the weight relationship between the pound scale and liquid measure is often close. Take a second and compare dry, liquid and avoirdupois weights and measures. For example, there are 16 fluid ounces in a pint and there are 16 ounces in a pound. There are 16 tablespoons to 1 cup and 16 cups to 1 gallon. The similarity is not, however, a true relationship. Two cups of flour weighs nearly nothing, while 2 cups of sugar weighs almost a pound and a pint jar of mercury weighs 17 pounds. It takes a little common sense. Most liquids are pretty close. Often, a recipe that calls for 1 fluid ounce can be measured quickly by filling 2 tablespoons.

FINAL CANNING NOTES

This information applies to all recipes in this book. There is a sidebar in each recipe that contains *Canning Notes*. These tell what type of canning—hot pack or water bath—will be needed and whether the recipe is acid, sugar saturated or acidified. Line two gives the pH that can be anticipated; and, if it is not where it should be, what to do about it. Number three tells how many jars the recipe will make. If there is a fluid ounce measurement stated first and then the number of jars, this means the size of jar is totally optional. Some folks want quarts of soup while others are content with pints. If a recipe states a single size jar, that is usually the one best suited for the task. Note number four tells the preparer whether the recipe can be cut in half or doubled. When reducing a recipe by half, it is often most wise to state each measurement in the smallest measure and then divide. For example, reduce pounds to ounces, tablespoons to teaspoons, etc. Sometimes there is a fifth note. This one is specifically for water bath products and states the weight of the principal ingredient in each jar. Knowing that each jar contains a specific weight of product, one can then shop or pick accordingly.

Under the ingredients section, measurements that are stated in dry or fluid quantities are the amounts that go into the pot. When an ingredient is stated in pounds, it is an unprepared weight, the weight before peeling, cutting, coring, etc. This is done to make planning and purchasing easier. To calculate buying four cups of chopped tomato is difficult at best and often leads to waste.

The second to last sentence in each recipe states "hot pack (or water bath) according to safe canning practices outlined on page 51!" Safe canning practices means:

1. Jars and lids have been sterilized.
2. The jars have been filled to the canning line.
3. Initial pH has been taken and the product is safe.
4. The temperature has been taken and it is at or above recommendation. Or, for water bathing, the stated temperature has been obtained and a 2-minute hold period has been timed.
5. The finished jars will be inverted for a minimum of 2 minutes.
6. After 24 hours, a test jar will be pH tested if the product is acidified.

These six steps are important and insure a degree of safety never before available to the home canner.

PART TWO

the recipes

WITH THE SUN climbing northward, warming a land cold from its winter retreat, I'll highlight each month and the crops that the sun brings to the South Carolina Lowcountry. The month described for a harvest here might not bring the same harvest in the region where you live, but the growing orders are probably similar. With a few exceptions, I have refrained from using recipes that include exotic fruits and vegetables not grown locally, and most are time-honored recipes made with local fare that has graced southern tables and pantries for over 150 years.

If a specific fresh ingredient is not available from a local grower in your part of the country, it can be had. It might not be as fresh as from the field where you just picked tomatoes or where you stocked up this morning at a local stand, but it will still be fresh enough to make a product that is many, many times better than anything commercially produced.

january

THE SEASON OF FESTIVITIES has ended. Except for fields of winter crops like collards, kale, mustard and turnips, the majority are protected from wind and weather with cover crops. What better time to take stock, to look over equipment and decide what needs to be purchased, replaced or upgraded, to ferret out new recipes and to plan the new canning year by product and quantity? This is a most important month. By late spring the canning calendar can keep us so busy we begin to react instead of plan. But just to stay in the groove, here's a recipe that requires little fresh produce and what is needed can readily be purchased at any grocery store. The recipe is an excellent one to test all the skills you perfected after a first year of learning.

lowcountry pluff mud

We named this product after the soft, squishy mud found everywhere around the Lowcountry at the low water mark. The muck is an ugly brown, and it reeks of organic decay. It is not a very appetizing name, but since the finished product looks so similar to the stuff that my brother and I bogged through as children at low tide, I could not help the moniker.

My son and I first learned to make this bean curd while sailing off the west coast of Mexico on our tiny sailboat headed for South Carolina. When we would go ashore to provision, curious locals, accustomed to rich Americans on big yachts, would ask how we managed. Our standard answer was that we fished. "Just in case," one person offered, and she gave us her family recipe for *refritos negros*; the idiom translates, refried black beans. A hundred miles further south another family volunteered their recipe saying the folks up north "Don't know beans about beans when it comes to beans." This scenario repeated itself many times.

By the time we cleared with the Port Captain in Puerto Madero, the southernmost Mexican port, we had mixed all the bean recipes and had a concoction that was, as they say, to die for. Still, it was complicated to make and fish were plentiful. Then one day, with a fair wind on our stern quarter, a warm sun in front of us, and two fishing lines trailing aft, Tom commented, "I hope we don't catch a fish today." And so began a bean fest that many nights fed us in the Pacific, the Caribbean and the Atlantic.

This is by far the most time consuming and most complicated canning one might ever undertake, but trust me, it is worth it. The finished product provides the main ingredient for a wonderful dip and an even better casual supper served over rice. This is something you will want in your pantry. It is so good in fact, that I have provided measurements so you can make six half pints to use as hors d'oeuvres, as well as five pints and four quarts to use as suppers for two and four persons. As a hors d'oeuvre, this attractive presentation makes a "hit of the party" dip. Heat the jar contents in a pot or microwave in the jar, lid removed, until very warm. Pour onto a plate or platter. On top of the mud, generously layer grated cheddar or one of the grated multi cheeses ubiquitously available. I am partial to the Mexican four cheese variety. On top of this, ladle a nice salsa, maybe even one you made. As a final topping, add a big dollop of rich sour cream. Have a bowl nearby with chips and stand by, ready to replenish. This goes faster than some plays in the Super Bowl—which happens to be an excellent and timely opportunity to debut this product. As a casual but complete meal, start with a bed of rice and then, following the procedures for the dip, build a supper. Sometimes I'll add some chicken sprinkled with cumin and chili powder that I have either baked or sautéed in olive oil. For an even more casual meal, food on the run, or supper on *Cinco de Mayo*, I mix equal parts of mud and rice together, spoon onto an open flour tortilla—the larger the better—and then add the cheese, salsa and sour cream; chicken is optional. Fold up the works and serve. What a May fifth celebration, what a burrito!

- **This is a hot pack, acidified recipe.**
- **Initial pH must be below 4.2.**
- **The recipe makes approximately 2 gallons; jar sizes are optional.**
- **The recipe can be doubled or halved.**

INGREDIENTS

6 pounds black beans, dry
4 pounds onions, diced and divided into approximately two equal portions
3 tablespoons garlic, minced and divided into two equal portions
$^1/_4$ pound jalapeño peppers, unseeded, diced fine and divided into two equal portions
3 tablespoons cumin
$^1/_2$ cup chili powder
3 quarts chicken stock*
$1^1/_2$ pounds salted butter (6 sticks)
5 bay leaves
$1^1/_2$ teaspoons salt
$1^1/_2$ tablespoons coarse-ground pepper
$^3/_4$ cup white sugar
3 cups lemon juice
$1^1/_2$ teaspoons citric acid (available wherever canning supplies are sold)

Wash the dried beans and place in a big pot covered by 2 inches of water. Bring to a strong boil. Boil for 10 minutes, stirring frequently.

Turn off heat. Allow beans to sit overnight. Next day, return to a boil. Remove from heat source when boiling begins. Rinse beans well under running water until water runs clear; drain.

To the pot with beans, add half the onions, half the garlic, half the jalapeños and all the cumin, chili powder and stock. Over medium heat, stirring often to prevent burning on the bottom, cook until beans are very tender and breaking up, about 2 to 3 hours. Firm beans will not can.

Melt butter in a separate pot and add to it the remaining vegetables. Cook over medium heat, stirring often, until the onions are clear.

When beans are soft, remove pot from heat. Take out half the beans and all the liquid, reserving some liquid for possible use later.

Purée the removed beans in a food processor or mash with a potato masher or pestle, adding some of the reserved liquid, a little at a time, to create a consistency that is thick and just able to pour, like oatmeal. Return to pot.

Add cooked vegetables with butter to the pot of beans and mix well. Return pot to stove over medium-high heat. Add balance of ingredients; bring to a low boil, stirring often.

Conduct initial pH test. To reduce to pH 4.2, add citric acid 1/4 teaspoon at a time.

Hot pack at 210 degrees F according to the safe canning practices outlined on page 51. Perform final pH testing after 24 hours to insure safe canning was accomplished and the pH is below 4.5.

*There are many types of chicken stock. Try to find the lower sodium kind. I use cubes mixed with water. The purist cooks will make their own!

types of **canning**

There are three types of canning: acidic, acidified and low acid. *Acidic* means that what is being preserved has acid properties enough to thwart the growth of specific bacteria. This group includes most preserves and plain fruits. *Acidified* is a class where the ingredients include certain introduced acids or acidic ingredients, like fruit or fruit juice, to render a recipe acidic. *Low acid*, mentioned earlier, is done in a pressure cooker. Pressure canning is a science unto itself. The same bacteria that acids render harmless in the first two methods must be killed by applying high heat for long periods. Pressure, temperature and time are all critical in the process. By the time the bacteria is neutralized so are many subtle flavors; consequently, pressure canning will not be addressed.

The two methods used to put up acidic and acidified products are the hot pack and water bath methods. In hot packing, the prepared and cooked product is poured into sterile canning jars and the jars are sealed. With water bathing, raw product is stuffed into jars, the jars are put in the special canning rack, hot liquid is poured into the jars, lids are loosely screwed on and the rack is lowered into boiling water. When a specific temperature is reached, the jars are removed and the lids are tightened. While each method serves a specific need for filling jars, both achieve a common end result of attaining a canning temperature that, based upon acidity, insures no pathogens will grow and an adequate preserving vacuum will be attained.

To begin your canning day, clear the areas, counters and stove where you plan to work and put out the equipment and utensils you will need. Next, wash and rinse the canning jars in warm water or run them through a dish washer. After they are clean and well rinsed, fill a sink with water and add 2 tablespoons of sodium hypoclorite (bleach) to each gallon of water. The mixture creates a two hundred part per million solution, enough to sterilize the canning jars and lids. Put enough water in the sink so the jars can stand upright and still be covered. Submerge the jars and lids, making sure there are no bubbles inside which might prevent complete sterilization. Using a clean dishcloth or sponge, wet with the same solution, wipe down all working surfaces. Keep the cloth handy; you will need it again. Remove the jars and place them upside down to drain. You are now ready for canning.

— february —

THE FIRST CROPS of the year are in the ground. One will be cut near the end of this month, so it won't be long. If the weather cooperates, asparagus plants will poke their heads up by mid February. Cutting will begin later and, with fair weather, one will be able to pickle a few spears near the end of the month. The harvest of Jerusalem artichokes begins in November; however, like potatoes, an incubation period concentrates the sugars, adding to the quality. By February, perfection can be achieved. If you are ready to begin, try your hand with these two main ingredients. I have selected the first recipe because few of us or the farmers we know grow a lot of garlic, yet garlic is readily available through wholesalers, food brokers and stores year-round.

Garlic Pickle
2/12/07

pickled garlic, hot pickled garlic, or fiery pickled garlic

One can find bulk, peeled garlic at warehouse stores like Sam's Club or Costco, although the more expensive garlic grown in Gilroy, California, the self-proclaimed "garlic capital of the world," is the best. With garlic, globalization has found its way into our food sources and our stomachs. This is a simple recipe, but it is so good you might find yourself making it over and over again throughout the year. It is quick and easy to produce and can be done in any season. Garlic is a heart healthy product. Many people swallow a clove a day; many more probably should!

Although I do not know the effect pickling has on garlic's medicinal properties, I can tell you this: because of ensuing breath challenges, very few salads include garlic cloves. It is often the missing flavor. This will change in your household because the pickled product does not affect one's breath. Mince a few cloves and add them to the greens. For parties, simply skewer the larger cloves on toothpicks and put out on a plate as an hors d'oeuvre. You will never find a clove remaining when tidying up. As a mid-afternoon snack or as a party finger food, one can crush the tender pickles with the back of a spoon and spread the paste on crackers. And here is the pièce de résistance; it comes after the garlic is gone. Save the liquid! To the liquid in the jar add an equal amount of white vinegar and half that amount of olive oil. Eyeball measuring is good enough. Shake well before using this exceptionally flavorful salad dressing.

CANNING NOTES

- This is a water bath, acidified recipe.
- The pH is low. Final pH will be below 4.
- The solution will fill 6 pint jars. It can be doubled or halved.
- Each jar requires about $3/4$ pound of fresh garlic.

IN EACH JAR

$1/2$ teaspoon celery seed
1 jalapeño pepper, split in half lengthwise for Hot Pickled Garlic only or 1 habañero pepper, slit open on one side for Fiery Pickled Garlic only
Fill jar with garlic, fresh and blanched

THE SOLUTION

3 pints white vinegar (5 percent acidity)
2 cups white sugar
2 tablespoons red pepper flakes
$1^1/2$ tablespoons salt

Load jars with celery seed and optional peppers.

Blanch garlic by submerging in boiling water for exactly 1 minute; drain well and pack jars tight with garlic up to canning line.

Bring vinegar to a boil. Add sugar, red pepper flakes and salt; stir well. Pour boiling solution (stirred to distribute red pepper flakes) over garlic until covered, filling center jar first. Loosely place lids on jars.

Test pH of liquid in center jar. Below 4.3 is fine, but if above, vinegar has incorrect acidity, discard and begin again with 5-percent acidity vinegar.

Water bath to 185 degrees F according to the safe canning practices outlined on page 51.

Perform final pH testing after 24 hours by crushing a clove of garlic in distilled water to insure pickle has been safely canned with a pH level below 4.5.

jerusalem **artichokes**

Contrary to the name, these tubers are not artichokes and they are not from Jerusalem. They are the root stock of a type of sunflower. The edible tuber grows like a potato. Unearthed, these "sunchokes" as they are often called, look much like gingerroot. They possess an earthy, nutty taste and make a delicious, crisp main ingredient for condiments. Interestingly, the Jerusalem artichoke is one of only a handful of vegetables native to the North American continent. The Indians were cultivating the plants by the time the first settlers stepped off the boat and balanced on Plymouth Rock. Consequently, we find many artichoke recipes dating to early colonial times.

One word of caution about artichokes: many a back yard farmer has planted a small patch of these prolific plants only to discover that by the following year or so they had overtaken the entire garden. One may ask, "Why is the south not covered by sunflowers instead of kudzu?" We began producing recipes using locally grown tubers, but in the second year a soil fungus attacked the tubers before maturity. This is nature's way.

There is a market for artichokes. For one reason, diabetics can eat cooked artichokes as a potato substitute because the starch is complex. As more bad press develops about the potato and links to type II diabetes, the nearly unknown Jerusalem artichoke might become even more available. If you don't grow them, or know of a farmer who does, you'll probably be able to find them in the store. I often see 2-pound sacks on the shelf at Whole Foods, a national grocer with a conscience. Your grocery store or fresh food distributor can procure Jerusalem artichokes.

The artichoke crop is dug in November, but it is the refrigerated incubation period that really sweetens them as liquids inside the tuber evaporate, concentrating the natural sugars. Consequently, local or store-bought chokes will be equal in quality. By February, it is high sunchoke time.

The major challenge in processing the artichoke is in the cleaning. The gnarly exterior creates tiny havens to trap dirt. Hearty washing and scrubbing is necessary to ensure the finished product is not gritty. Many families in the South wash their artichokes in the washing machine. They are tough enough to stand the abuse of the oscillating paddles while slowly giving up the grit.

artichoke pickles

My first recollection of artichoke pickles was of my parents serving them at a cocktail party. As I passed by the table heading for the kitchen, they caught my eye and I plucked one into my mouth. I made fourteen additional trips to the kitchen that night. I cannot remember if any of the guests ever tasted one of my grandmother's delights. I sure did and I've been hooked ever since. The alum in the recipe is used to make the pickles crisp. I buy small boxes at local drug stores like Rite-Aid and Eckerd's. Sometimes they have to order it and it takes a few days, so plan ahead.

CANNING NOTES
- **This is a water bath, acidified recipe.**
- **pH is low. Final pH will be below 4.**
- **The solution will fill 6 pint jars. Half pints are ineffective, but quarts work.**
- **One can make as many jars as is practical.**
- **Each jar will require approximately $1/2$ pound artichokes.**

VEGETABLES
3 pounds Jerusalem artichokes, scrubbed, skinned, shaped and twice soaked
1 red bell pepper, diced large
1 onion, diced large

FIRST SOAK
$1/2$ cup salt
$1/2$ gallon water

SECOND SOAK
$1/4$ cup alum
$1/2$ gallon water

PICKLING SOLUTION
1 quart vinegar (5 percent acidity)
$1^1/4$ pounds sugar
1 tablespoon salt
$1/2$ tablespoon celery seed
1 teaspoon turmeric

Prepare the chokes by washing, shaping and then scrubbing off the outer dark coating (I use a pot scrubber). Using a paring knife, I like to form various smooth shapes no bigger than a thumb.

Soak the prepared artichokes in the salt solution, refrigerated, for 24 hours. Rinse well and soak in the alum solution, refrigerated, for at least 24 hours.

Prepare pickling solution and bring to a boil. Remove artichokes from alum solution but do not rinse.

Load each sterile pint jar with 1 tablespoon bell pepper and 1 tablespoon onion, and then pack well, up to the canning line, with prepared artichokes.

Put jars in canning rack. Artichokes will darken when exposed to air for long periods, so work steadily.

Pour boiling pickling solution over artichokes until covered.

Conduct initial pH test of liquid. If not below 4, the vinegar was not correct or another liquid was accidentally used. Discard liquid and begin again.

Water bath to 182 degrees F according to safe canning practices outlined on page 51.

Perform final pH testing after 24 hours by crushing an artichoke pickle in distilled water after rinsing in distilled water.

NOTE: It is important not to exceed the prescribed temperature or hold time as pickles will lose their crispness and will get mushy.

artichoke relish

This delightful, sweet relish has been a mainstay of our canning career, contributing much to our success. My partner and son, Tom, has an excellent palate. With twenty recipes before us, we mixed and matched while we cooked. Tom would say "add a little of this, add more, we still need more, okay that's perfect." Then on to the next ingredient; add more, more, stop; and so on until we had the recipe below. Popularity was explosive. Following the introduction we made over twenty-four hundred jars a month. That was ten years ago. Its acceptance continues to this day. Part of the popularity of this relish comes from its diverse usage. First used as a side for greens, this sweet earthy, nutty dressing has matured into an additive to make almost anything better. People report adding a little dollop to deviled eggs or coleslaw, and some even slather a layer on top of broiled or baked fish. Of course, one can use it like any other relish, on hamburgers and hot dogs, or as an hors d'oeuvre by simply pouring some over cream cheese and offering it with water crackers. A whole generation of children in Mt. Pleasant and Charleston demand tuna fish sandwiches instead of peanut butter and jelly because of the artichoke relish added to the salad.

CANNING NOTES
- **This is a hot pack, acidified recipe.**
- **Both initial and final pH will be below 4.**
- **The recipe makes 10 pint jars or 19 half pints.**
- **The recipe can be halved or doubled.**

SOAK
1 cup salt
1 gallon water

VEGETABLES
5 pounds Jerusalem artichokes, diced or chopped in processor
2 1/2 pounds onions, diced
1 1/4 pounds green bell pepper, diced
3/4 pound red bell pepper, diced

SOLUTION
2 1/2 tablespoons turmeric
3/4 cup flour
1 to 1 1/2 quarts white vinegar (5 percent acidity), divided
3 1/2 pounds sugar
1/2 cup mustard seed
2 1/2 tablespoons celery seed

Dissolve salt in water, add vegetables and soak for 24 hours, refrigerated. Rinse vegetables twice and allow to fully drain in colander.

Make a smooth, runny paste with the turmeric, flour and 2 cups vinegar.

Put a pot over medium-high heat with remaining vinegar. Add sugar and stir to dissolve. Add the prepared paste and the mustard and celery seeds; mix well.

Mix in the vegetables, stirring often to prevent burning. As the temperature rises, the flour will begin to thicken and the mixture will darken.

Maintain a low boil for 10 minutes after darkening. Add water, 1/4 cup at a time, if the relish becomes too thick. Achieve the consistency of pancake batter.

Conduct initial pH test to insure a safe level that is below 4.2. If necessary to lower pH, add additional vinegar 2 tablespoons at a time.

Hot pack above 200 degrees F according to the safe canning practices outlined on page 51.

Perform final pH testing after 24 hours to insure safe canning was accomplished and the pH is below 4.5.

artichoke chow-chow

Where the name chow-chow originated seems to be shrouded among history's mysteries. I have my own uneducated theory about its origins. As I peruse recipes I sometimes see cabbage in relishes but I almost always see cabbage as a main ingredient in chow-chow. The French Protestant diaspora created by the revocation of the edict of Nantes in 1685 brought Huguenots in droves to this country, many settling in the Lowcountry. Names like Horry, (pronounced O-ree), and Porcher (pronounced Pachee), command great respect, three hundred years later. The French word for cabbage is choux! A coincidence? "Bingo!"—a relish called cabbage food. I passed my grass roots concept by a food historian who blew me off with a wave, as if to say that I was out of my league. I'm sure I am, but I'll stick with my unsupported theory and let the academicians debate chow-chow origins along with the number of angels that can sit on the head of a pin.

CANNING NOTES
- **This is a hot pack, acidified recipe.**
- **The final pH will be below 4.**
- **The recipe makes 6 pint jars or 12 half pints.**
- **The recipe can be doubled.**

INGREDIENTS
$2^1/_2$ pounds Jerusalem artichokes, diced
$1^1/_2$ pounds cabbage, chopped
1 pound onions, diced
$^1/_2$ pound red bell pepper, diced
$^1/_2$ pound green bell pepper, diced
$1^1/_2$ cups sugar
4 teaspoons salt
4 teaspoons whole celery seed
$^1/_3$ cup flour
2 tablespoons mustard powder
1 tablespoon turmeric
3 cups vinegar, divided (5 percent acidity)

Prepare, measure and place in a pot all ingredients except flour, mustard powder, turmeric and half the vinegar.

Make a smooth, runny paste with the flour, mustard and one-fourth of the remaining vinegar. Add paste to pot and mix well.

Withhold the remaining vinegar until mixture begins to thicken, then add as needed to make the consistency of pancake batter.

Bring to a boil, stirring often.

Conduct initial pH test. If not below 4.2 add additional vinegar $^1/_4$ cup at a time.

Hot pack above 200 degrees F according to the safe canning practices outlined on page 51.

Perform final pH test after 24 hours to insure safe canning was accomplished and the pH is below 4.5.

lots of **"chow-chow"**

Today, in America, there are almost as many chow-chow recipes as there are small towns. Among the seasons of this book, you will find three great ones. The first is artichoke. The traditional southern table has not only its courses, but to sweeten the pot further, one enviably finds a condiment for each. We sought the earthy flavor of the sunchoke less the sweetness of the relish, so we turned to our personal collection of cookbooks, many of which were bequeathed by "Pinky" Haynsworth. It was her grandfather who, on January 11, 1861, fired a cannon ball across the bow of *The Star of the West*, the first hostility in "The War of Northern Aggression." The abundance of cookbooks started with the Charleston Junior League publishing the first of its kind in 1950. The book, *Charleston Receipts*, is now in its thirtieth printing. It has been imitated by a host of similar, league, town and church-spun books. I own a whole shelf full, most of them from South Carolina. This is the land called the Bible Belt, and yet for the life of me, I never knew there were so many churches, much less so many denominations. By mixing recipes from ten of these books we developed the Artichoke Chow-Chow.

Many folks prefer this recipe over the Artichoke Relish (see page 67) as the accompaniment to greens because it is not sweet. I use either and also enjoy this chow-chow when I am serving rich, red meats like lamb or beef. The cabbage renders an acerbic taste while the artichokes lend an earthy, nutty flavor like one would find in a forest. It is a perfect complement to the twenty-first century version of a hunter's feast.

march

THERE ARE FEW LIONS parading in with March and any rawness that was February has begun to fade. Winter winds still blow on occasion, but when the clouds expose the sun its warmth reminds us of just how close we are to that imaginary arc encircling the globe at latitude 23.7 N degrees, the circle that separates us from the tropics. The turned earth welcomes the heat once again and the seeds already in the ground are taking firm root. Renewal of life is under way. Farmers begin to check rain gauges, praying for a world that is like e. e. cummings' "puddle wonderful." It doesn't take long before a new green coat begins to paint over a brown landscape. By the middle of the month comes the first of the spring produce. Asparagus fills fields in perfusion and if one has not already begun pickling some of the tender spears, now is the time.

strawberry preserves

The standard applications of strawberry preserves are well known: a spread on toast, biscuits or muffins and, of course, cornbread in the South. But why leave this delectable for only the breakfast table? Spoon a dollop over a scoop of vanilla ice cream for a dessert treat. For an out-of-the-ordinary, try this: When my granddaughter, Ashley, comes to visit, I make her what my mother calls, *oef au confiture*. Sounds fancy? It isn't. Our translation is, a cream cheese and strawberry preserve omelet. Once the egg begins to firm, add a small cut of cream cheese and a tablespoon or two of your homemade preserves, fold over the omelet and let the cheese soften. For the little three year old it is always a highlight. For me too, on both counts!

CANNING NOTES

- This is a hot pack, acid recipe.
- pH is not an issue. No testing is required.
- This recipe makes 7-plus pints or 15 half pints. Jar size cannot exceed pint size.
- The recipe can be halved but not doubled.

INGREDIENTS

10 plus cups strawberries, capped and quartered
  (4 quarts whole berries)
1/2 cup lemon juice (fresh squeezed is better)
2 packs pectin (or 2/3 cup bulk pectin)
1 tablespoon butter
14 cups sugar, divided

Prepare ingredients and place all but sugar in a pot; mix well. On high heat, stirring often, bring to a rolling boil.

When boil can no longer be stirred down, add half the sugar and mix well. When pot begins to boil a second time, add balance of sugar and mix well. Stirring continuously, bring to a full rolling boil. Hold rolling boil for 3 minutes. Test for jelling after 2 minutes.

Hot pack according to the safe canning practices outlined on page 51.

NOTE: Stir the ingredients well as you ladle into jars so each jar gets an equal portion of whole fruit. I use two equal size measures of the same capacity as the jars I'm filling. One hangs on the inside edge of the pot for scooping from the pot and one for filling the jar. This keeps the mess down and insures an equal amount of whole fruit in each jar. Once in the jars, the chunks float to the top. After the 2-minute inverted requirement,

right the jars and over the next 30 minutes or so, periodically check. Shake the jars to disperse the particulates uniformly until jelling sets the fruit.

VARIATION:
STRAWBERRY CINNAMON PRESERVES

Even your world-class preserves will become commonplace in time. After all, you have raised the bar. Your family will forget how full of flavor your preserves are when compared to store bought. Here is a mix and match suggestion to add that touch of diversity. Make these preserves exactly as you would the regular strawberry preserves above, but in addition to the initial ingredients that go in the pot, add a cinnamon stick for each jar. Just before you are ready to can, when the rolling boil has begun and the 3-minute timer is ticking, place 1 cinnamon stick in each canning jar. Fill and invert jars in the prescribed manner.

strawberries

Of the many fruits that come each spring and summer, the strawberry is my favorite to preserve. Most times I wait for the hot sun of April to sweeten them, but in good years, I make a few jars in March. To achieve world-class flavor, it is important to meet three conditions, and a fourth is desirable.

1. Strawberries must be picked ripe. Touch each berry. If the fruit falls off the vine, it becomes an excellent candidate for canning. There should be no green or white patches on the berry.

2. Avoid picking if it has rained during the previous four days. The less rain during the maturation process the better.

3. Lastly, the hotter the days, the sweeter the berries. Unfortunately, this condition creates a double-edged sword since the South gets so hot that by the beginning of June the vines shrivel, the berries burn and the season ends.

4. Another desirable criteria is Visqueen, the ugly black or clear polyethylene sheeting. Growers lay the plastic over the rows of strawberry plants after planting. The why of doing this is unimportant, but to us, the preservers, the berries arrive in the canning kitchen much cleaner. At worst, they have specks of blown dust on their skins, nothing that a misting rinse won't take care of. The abundance of a strawberry's flavor lies in its outer layers. A good washing will clean off as much flavor as it will dirt.

Between March and June is the canning festival for things strawberry. There are no secrets to making world-class strawberry preserves other than the picking of the berries and the preparation of the fruit.

The instructions inside a pectin pack say never to double a recipe because it will not jell. There is chemistry behind this caveat. It has to do with the rapid reduction of heat created with the introduction of sugar. This damages the forming of the molecular jelling chains. We always run double measures, and to prevent the excessive reduction in heat, we take two precautionary steps. We use a pot with a large, heavy bottom and excellent conductivity—my Wal-Mart 12-quart pot. This gives a big, hot surface area. Second, we add half of the measured sugar, allow the pot to return to a minor boil, add the second half of sugar and then bring the ingredients to the required rolling boil. We learned this trick from the folks at Pacific Pectin.

pickled asparagus

I never am fond of pickling asparagus because so much of the plant is wasted to make the stalk fit into a pint jar, plus the vegetable is expensive. Still every pantry should have its complement of Pickled Asparagus. For the left over stalks, using only the tenderest of the sections, I first steam until soft and then purée the asparagus stems mixed with enough water to make a runny paste. For each cup of purée add 1 cup milk with 2 tablespoons flour mixed in well, and 1 cup cream. Add 1 tablespoon butter for each cup of purée, and add salt and pepper to taste and heat until the soup begins to thicken. Served either hot or chilled, cream of asparagus soup makes a great lunch or a pleasant first course. The pickled spears can be served as hors d'oeuvres or added to main course salads to give a new dimension.

CANNING NOTES

- **This is a water bath, acidified recipe.**
- **pH is low. Final pH will be below 4.**
- **Recipe solution fills 4 pint jars; wide mouth jars are easier to pack.**
- **One can make as many jars as practical.**
- **Approximately 1 pound of asparagus will be needed for each jar made.**

IN EACH JAR

1 pound asparagus, cut to length, blanched and packed tight

1 tablespoon chopped onion
1 teaspoon whole celery seed
1 slice lemon, peel on
$1/2$ teaspoon red pepper flakes (optional)
1 clove garlic

PICKLING SOLUTION

3 cups cider vinegar
3 cups water
7 tablespoons salt ($1/2$ cup less 1 tablespoon)

Measure length, cut and blanch asparagus in boiling water for 10 seconds.

Prepare jars and bring pickling solution to a boil.

Load jars, place in canning rack and fill with the boiling solution.

Take initial pH test of liquid. If above 4.2, improper mixture of vinegar and water or improper acidity of vinegar exists. Discard liquid and begin again.

Water bath to 185 degrees F according to the safe canning practices outlined on page 51.

Perform final pH testing after 24 hours by crushing an asparagus spear or macerating in a blender, with 1 cup distilled water to insure safe canning was accomplished and the pH is below 4.5.

april

THIS IS HARDLY T.S. Eliot's "cruelest of months." Of all the months, I recall Aprils with the fondest of memories. The air is dry, the days warm, the nights cool. The bright pastel colors of Easter are among us, both in the azaleas and in city folk dress. For every creature, including man, it is the season of courting. Wisteria gives a purple brush stroke to a land awaiting the resurrection celebration. Here comes a new world. In the fields the story is one of work. Fifty years ago, truck farmers were cutting cabbage. The heavily laden carts moved the heads to even heavier laden trucks that drove the produce to railheads. The land both north and south of Charleston smelled of turned earth and raw vegetables. That picturesque era is gone. Urban and suburban sprawl have all but ended the agrarian age.

The canning season has yet to really get under way. Still the few remaining farmers have their hands full tending and gathering crops, including asparagus, peas, beets, broccoli, cabbage, and all the greens still coming up, plus of course, strawberries, now luscious because of warm sunshine.

strawberry-orange marmalade

The word marmalade is old. The Portuguese sailed with marmalade in the ship's stores, for they already knew what would take the English another two hundred years to learn, that citrus wards off scurvy. The dreaded vitamin deficiency is not our plague. Our challenge is that not everyone is a marmalade fan. Some don't like the toughness of the rind, others the sour of lemon against the sweet. But for those that are marmalade aficionados, there is none better than Strawberry Orange. The two citruses, the rinds and the berries assemble as a quartet on one's palate. Although I would not recommend it, the citrus rinds can be removed when preparing the fruit.

CANNING NOTES

- **This is a hot pack, acid recipe.**
- **pH is not an issue. No testing is required.**
- **The recipe makes approximately 6 pints or 13 half pints.**
- **The recipe can be halved but not doubled. Jar size cannot exceed pint size.**

INGREDIENTS

5 plus cups strawberries, ripe, cleaned, topped and quartered (about 2 plus quarts)
4 oranges, thin skinned, thin sliced, then seeded and quartered
2 lemons, thin sliced, then seeded and quartered
1 cup water
$1/_2$ tablespoon butter
2 packs pectin (or $2/_3$ cup bulk pectin)
12 cups sugar, divided

Prepare ingredients and place all but sugar in a pot. Over high heat, stirring often or continuously, bring to a rolling boil.

Add half the sugar, mix well and stir until ingredients show signs of boiling. Add balance of sugar. Bring to a full, rolling boil, continuing to stir. Time boil for 3 minutes, but check for jelling after 2 minutes.

Take pot off heat and hot pack according to the safe canning practices outlined on page 51.

NOTE: Stir the ingredients well as you ladle into jars so each gets a portion of whole fruit. Once in the jars, the chunks of fruit float to the top. After the 2-minute inverted requirement, right the jars and over the next half hour or so, periodically check. Shake the jars to disperse the particulates uniformly until jelling sets the fruit throughout.

pickled beets

Beets are a strange one, but the flavors are so inviting in salads—especially the flavor of pickled beets. I could not help but include this simple but time-consuming recipe among the crops of April. Each pantry should have several pints.

CANNING NOTES
- **This is a water bath, acidified recipe.**
- **pH is low. Final pH will be below 4.**
- **The solution will fill 6 pint jars. Half pints are ineffective, but quarts work.**
- **One can make as many jars as is practical.**
- **Each pint jar will require approximately $3/4$ pound of beets.**

5 pounds small beets
1 quart vinegar (5 percent acidity)
$1^1/2$ tablespoons allspice, ground
6 cinnamon sticks
$1/4$ cup honey

With root left on and 2 inches of stem remaining, cover beets with water and boil.

When tender, put in cold water and peel. Cut beets into quarters or other shapes depending on size of beets.

Put all but beets and honey in a pot and bring to a boil; add honey.

Put beet chunks in jars and then fill with boiling liquid.

Conduct initial pH test of liquid to insure proper solution acidity. If pH is above 4.1, improper acidity of vinegar was used; discard liquid and begin again.

Water bath to 185 degrees F according to the safe canning practices outlined on page 51.

Perform final pH testing after 24 hours by crushing a section of beet in distilled water to insure safe canning was accomplished and the pH is below 4.5.

may

WE LIVE IN A mobile society. Many a newly arrived neighbor tells me he chose the Lowcountry because of the weather. The fact that we have four seasons and a temperate winter without the harsh cold that hangs for weeks or months makes it seem like nirvana for folks coming from northern climes. No place is perfect. Residents face the threat of hurricanes from July until November and the land sits atop a major seismic fault. When writing in the early mornings I often feel the slightest of tremors, just reminding me that even Charleston is not without fault!

And then there is the summer. July and August are stifling hot, even hotter now that tree cover has given way to housing tracts. But, today we have air conditioning. If there was one invention that made the Lowcountry a change of residence destination it was "air." Air conditioners or not, I could live here just because of May. The days are warm; a few might even remind us of what is coming, but the nights remain cool. The air is filled with the perfume scent of Confederate Jasmine, and to cap off what is already the divine ingredients of nature, man enjoins the beauty by bringing Spoleto Festival U.S.A., an exploration of the arts on a world-class level. It is difficult to remain fixed in a tiny kitchen with so many activities. So, I rise early, do my canning, and the rest of the day is for play. The month will see the last of the strawberries and cabbage and the first of the cucumbers and tomatoes, although still green. Work is picking up.

uncle patty's garlic pickles

This recipe works well under heat. Uncle Patty, a second generation American, created this recipe some years after working at his father's vegetable store. The store was across from The Old Citadel on Marion Square in Charleston. Patty's father was loved by cadets. The turn-of-the-century military students were forbidden to step from the school's boundaries, so either father or little Patty would run across the street to lend them money or give them fruit. Ever since Patty told me the story I have felt certain my grandfather was one of their patrons.

CANNING NOTES
- **This is a water bath, acidified recipe.**
- **pH will be below 4.**
- **The solution will fill 6 pint jars.**
- **One can make as many jars as is practical.**
- **Each jar will require approximately 1^1/$_2$ pounds of cucumbers.**

VEGETABLES
7^1/$_2$ pounds cucumbers

SOAK
1 gallon water
1 cup pickling lime

IN EACH JAR
2 jalapeño peppers, ends cut off and sliced in half lengthwise
4 cloves garlic, 2 minced and 2 whole
^{1}/$_2$ teaspoon dill seed

PICKLING SOLUTION
4 cups white vinegar (5 percent acidity)
2 cups water
^{3}/$_4$ cup sugar
^{1}/$_2$ cup salt
3 tablespoons Ball pickling mix (available in many grocery stores and where canning supplies are found)

Soak the unprepared, whole cucumbers in lime solution, refrigerated, for a minimum of 16 hours.

Upon completion of the soak, scrub the white film off the cucumbers. Trim both ends off each cucumber so that the length will fit the jar (4^1/$_4$ inches).

Slice each cucumber lengthwise into four equal-sized spears or more if the cucumbers are fat.

Fill the jars with jalapeño, garlic and dill, and then stuff as many cucumber spears as possible into each jar.

Mix the pickling solution and bring to a strong boil.

Place the jars in a canning rack and fill with boiling liquid.

Conduct initial pH test of liquid. If pH is below 4.2, it is fine. A pH above indicates a solution with too much water or improper acidity of vinegar was used. Discard liquid and begin again.

Water bath to 185 degrees F according to the safe canning practices outlined on page 51.

Perform final pH testing after 24 hours by chopping or macerating a section of pickle spear in distilled water to insure safe canning was accomplished and the pH is below 4.5.

green tomato chow-chow

Traditionally, chow-chows are on the table to ladle on top of mustard, turnip or collard greens. If that isn't southern, nothing is, and it sure beats just pouring vinegar over the top or plopping on a killer dollop of mayonnaise. One year when my mother invited us to Thanksgiving dinner, she asked if we had any special requests. "Do some greens," I said, "and I'll bring a jar of our chow-chow." That Thanksgiving it was helping after helping; the three of us nearly turned green, we ate so much. Old-time southerners really knew what they were doing. That Thanksgiving there was plenty of turkey left over for sandwiches to be made with Green Tomato Pickles on page 87.

CANNING NOTES
- **This is a hot pack, acidified recipe.**
- **Initial pH will be below 4.**
- **The recipe makes approximately 96 ounces or 6 pints.**
- **The recipe can be doubled.**

VEGETABLES
2^1/$_2$ pounds green tomatoes, chopped fine
1^1/$_2$ pounds green bell peppers, diced
3 pounds cabbage, cored and chopped
2 pounds yellow onions, diced

SOAK
^{1}/$_3$ cup salt
2 quarts boiling water

PICKLING SOLUTION
3 tablespoons all-purpose flour
2^1/$_2$ tablespoons Colman's mustard powder
5 cups cider vinegar
3^1/$_2$ cups sugar
3 tablespoons butter, melted
1^1/$_2$ tablespoons turmeric
2 tablespoons whole celery seed
1 tablespoons mustard seed

Prepare vegetables and place in soak solution until cool, about 4 hours; drain vegetables and wring out all fluid but do not rinse.

Mix with whisk or in a blender the flour, mustard powder and turmeric with 2 cups of the vinegar to make a smooth, runny paste.

Put drained produce in a pot with remaining ingredients and bring to a boil.

Allow flour to thicken and cabbage to cook, about 20 minutes.

Conduct initial pH test. Below 4.3 is fine. If above, reduce by adding vinegar 2 tablespoons at a time.

Hot pack above 190 degrees F according to the safe canning practices on page 51.

Perform final pH testing after 24 hours to insure safe canning was accomplished and pH is below 4.5.

bread and butter pickles

This cucumber recipe has been around for most of the twentieth century and its popularity has pushed it into the twenty-first. There are a couple of reasons why. The pickle is sweet and today, sweet rules. For the home canner, bread and butter pickles are easy to produce and the cucumbers do not have to be soaked in lime and then scrubbed clean, a deterrent to even a diehard "putting upper." Every pantry should hold a few jars for home use on burgers or sandwiches. And this classic pickle will be cherished as a gift.

CANNING NOTES
- **This is a hot pack, acidified recipe.**
- **Initial pH will be below 4.**
- **The recipe makes approximately 96 ounces or 8 pints.**
- **The recipe can be doubled or halved.**

INGREDIENTS
8 pounds small-sized cucumbers, sliced thin but not peeled

3 pounds white onions, chopped
2 green bell peppers, diced
4 cloves garlic, minced
$1/3$ cup salt
5 cups sugar
2 cups cider vinegar
$1^1/_2$ teaspoons turmeric
2 teaspoons celery seed
1 tablespoon mustard seed
1 teaspoon whole cloves

Prepare vegetables, and combine and sprinkle with salt; cover with chilled water. After 4 hours, drain well but do not rinse.

Combine all remaining ingredients except vegetables in a pot and bring to a boil.

Add vegetable mixture and return to a boil. Prepare to can immediately.

Conduct initial pH test. Below 4.2 is fine. If above, reduce by adding vinegar 2 tablespoons at a time.

Hot pack above 200 degrees F according to the safe canning practices outlined on page 51.

Perform final pH testing after 24 hours by crushing a slice of pickle in distilled water after rinsing in distilled water.

cucumbers

In days gone by, kitchens had a big, clay crock pot stashed in the corner. It was filled with seasoned brine or salted vinegar. As vegetables came in, some were added to the crock for pickling. This process served two purposes—making pickles and preserving vegetables out of season.

Not so long ago, in New York delicatessens, I would see big oak, brine-filled barrels where floating cucumbers slowly pickled. That era has passed. Government agencies would close down such a store within minutes, even though, through a thousand years of history, barrels like those made folks happy. Today, we put the heat to all that we used to pickle naturally.

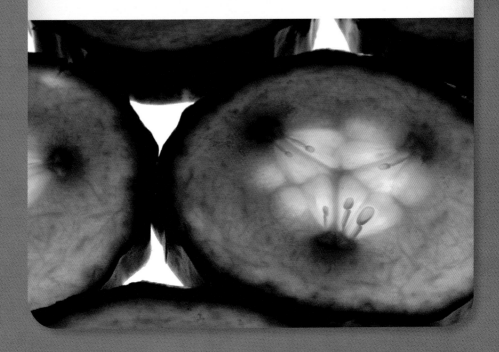

hot chow-chow

One has to have a few delectables that spice up their pantry, and this is a favorite. There is only so much space on the tables at the farmers market because sampling is the key to selling. Once someone tastes, if they like, they become a customer for life. Chow-Chow was never a great seller, so I used the space for more sought after items. Still a week never went by without the question "Do you have any chow-chow?" Then, four weeks in a row I was asked if I had a hot chow-chow. I retired to the drafting kitchen.

The first four takes got thrown away. The fifth had promise. The sixth was good. I don't eat a lot of meat and I try to refrain entirely from processed foods, but I either have little conviction or was hungry because I thought, what better way to test this hot chow-chow than on a hot dog and bun? My first revelation was that one can now actually purchase an equal number of dogs and buns. By the time I was home the experimental recipe had cooled. On the bun I smeared a little mayonnaise, positioned the doggie, ladled on the chow-chow and ate. I couldn't believe it. The simple Coney Island fast food was like a gourmet meal—sweet, hot and rich. I consumed six of the eight hot dogs and spent the rest of the afternoon sitting like a Buddha, but too full to contemplate my belly or my new market coup.

CANNING NOTES
- **This is a hot pack, acidified recipe.**
- **Initial pH will be below 4.**
- **The recipe makes approximately 96 ounces or 6 pints.**
- **The recipe can be doubled.**

SOAK SOLUTION
$3/4$ gallon boiling water
$3/4$ cup salt

VEGETABLES
1 medium red cabbage, chopped
$2^1/2$ pounds ripe red tomatoes, cored and chopped

1 pound red bell peppers, diced
1 pound serrano or other hot, red peppers, chopped but not seeded
$1^1/2$ pounds sweet onions, chopped fine

PICKLING SOLUTION
3 tablespoons Colman's dry mustard
6 tablespoons all-purpose flour
1 tablespoon turmeric
3 cups cider vinegar, divided
$2^1/4$ cups sugar
2 tablespoons celery seed
2 tablespoons mustard seed
$1/4$ cup butter ($1/2$ stick)

Prepare soak solution and then pour over vegetables and let stand for 12 hours. Drain well, then rinse vegetables once to remove some of the salted water.

Make a smooth paste of mustard powder, flour and turmeric with 1 cup of the vinegar. Add all ingredients to the pot and bring to a boil. Reduce heat and cook 20 minutes.

Conduct initial pH test. If pH is below 4.3 it is fine. To reduce, add additional vinegar 2 tablespoons at a time.

Hot pack above 200 degrees F in according to safe canning practices outlined on page 51.

Perform final pH testing after 24 hours to insure safe canning was accomplished and the pH is below 4.5.

green tomato pickle

I used to place a slice of these sweetened sour pickles on the dinner plate to separate fried chicken from rice. The other division was with mustard greens. This gave a balanced presentation. One customer of ours, an ancient granny, ordered four jars of Green Tomato Pickle every month. Like clockwork, when the calendar struck the eighth, she ordered. I finally asked what she did with all those slices. "Oh," she said, "for lunch I place a slice or two on my sandwich along with sliced turkey." Her comments changed my life and my waistline. Each day, Lila, chief of the kitchen, at lunchtime would make me a turkey sandwich with a slice of green tomato pickle. Life's simplest pleasures are often the best.

CANNING NOTES
- **This is a water bath, acidified recipe.**
- **pH is low. Final pH will be below 4.**
- **The solution will fill 6 pint jars.**
- **One can make as many jars as is practical.**
- **Each jar will require approximately 2 or 3 small green tomatoes.**

PICKLING SOLUTION
2 cups vinegar (5 percent acidity)
4^1/$_2$ cups sugar

IN EACH JAR
1 teaspoon whole celery seed
2 tablespoons diced-fine onion
^{1}/$_2$ teaspoon whole mustard seed
^{1}/$_2$ teaspoon dill seed
3 peppercorns
1 clove garlic
Slices of green tomato

Heat vinegar to boiling and dissolve sugar in solution.

Fill jars and pour in the solution, insuring all air pockets are removed. (I slide a butter knife down the inside of the jar to make a channel for the liquid to flow.)

Conduct initial pH test of liquid in center jar. If pH is 4.2, it is fine. Higher means incorrect acidity vinegar was used. If so, discard liquid and begin again.

Water bath to 183 degrees F according to the safe canning practices outlined on page 51.

Perform final pH testing after 24 hours to insure safe canning was accomplished and the pH is below 4.5.

very berry preserves

Near the end of May or by the first of June there is often a moment when all of the season's berries are ripe; some at the end of their run like strawberries and others just beginning. When the ripe fruits coalesce, about once every three years, it is the opportunity to make this popular and unique preserve. Of course, in this day of fast delivery, if one fruit is not vine ready it can be found. For best results, just make sure store-bought berries are sweet.

CANNING NOTES

- **This is a hot pack, acid recipe.**
- **pH is not an issue. No testing is required.**
- **This recipe makes 10 half pints.**
- **The recipe should not be altered.**

INGREDIENTS

3 cups crushed strawberries
1$^1/_2$ cups crushed red raspberries
1$^1/_2$ cups crushed blueberries
$^1/_4$ cup lemon juice
1 tablespoon butter
1 pack pectin or $^1/_3$ cup bulk pectin
8$^1/_2$ cups sugar

Prepare, measure and place all ingredients except sugar in a pot; mix well. Over high heat, stirring often, bring to a rolling boil.

When boil can no longer be stirred down, add the sugar and mix well.

Now stirring continuously, bring to a full, rolling boil.

Hold rolling boil for at least 1 minute and then test for jelling.

Hot pack according to the safe canning practices on page 51.

june

THIS IS THE FIRST of the two biggest months in Lowcountry farming, with about nineteen crops coming to harvest. There was a time, not so long ago, when, in June, kitchen lights came on at 3 am. An hour later, even before first light, the fields were crowded with workers. By daybreak the skies were again darkened, this time by dust as tractors ran up and down the rows, cutting, beating or digging. By 11 am, the sun had gotten the best of even the hardiest, so work shut down. Farmers relaxed with iced tea on screened porches until dinner, the midday meal in the South served at 1 pm. An hour or so afterwards, the fierce heat began to subside. Then it was back to the fields, digging, cutting or picking. Activities went on until dark. Today, many of the old farms and fields are housing subdivisions. Most of the farmers are gone. A few hold out. God bless them.

green tomato relish

There are many recipes for this wonderful fruit. I started in May with a few green tomato recipes and then began to add some red since that is what happens on the vine. I have included in the June section mostly red tomato recipes where the sweet juices of a just picked ripe tomato are primary and dominate the recipe. I continue with additional tomato recipes during the summer months because of other predominant ingredients just coming out of the fields and while top-quality tomatoes are still available regionally, if not locally.

   In the agrarian society that was the Old South, the Lowcountry was best known for Carolina Gold rice. Up and down the coast, a hundred miles in both directions, plantation homes were surrounded by fields of gold shimmering among summer breezes. The tiny grain brought a wealth to the region and its planters that was unheralded in the eighteenth century and made Charleston a significant cultural center within the young nation. It is often said, in jest, that Charlestonians are like the Chinese in that they eat rice and worship their ancestors. With so many rice dishes and even a special silver rice spoon to serve it, one can imagine the number of adjectives that have been created over three hundred years to accent the bland tasting, whitish starch. Green Tomato Relish is a classic. The sweet and vinegary fixin' spooned over top, will turn the little white mound on one's plate into an orchestra of unforgettable flavors.

CANNING NOTES
- **This is a hot pack, acidified recipe.**
- **The pH will be below 4.**
- **The recipe makes approximately 6 pint jars.**
- **The recipe can be doubled.**

VEGETABLES
5 pounds green tomatoes, diced
3 large red bell peppers, diced
1 pound sweet onions, diced
2 jalapeño peppers, chopped
1/2 cup salt

BOILING SOLUTION
2 tablespoons mustard seed
2 tablespoons celery seed
1 pound sugar
4 cups vinegar (5 percent acidity), divided

Prepare vegetables, sprinkle with salt and allow to set overnight.

   Drain vegetables well but do not rinse. Put vegetables in a pot with seeds, sugar and half the vinegar.

   At 190 degrees F, add additional vinegar 1/2 cup at a time as necessary to keep relish wet, but don't allow mixture to become runny. Return mixture to 190 degrees F.

   Conduct initial pH test. If pH is 4.3, it is fine. To reduce, add vinegar 2 tablespoons at a time.

   Hot pack at 190 degrees F according to the safe canning practices on page 51.

   Perform final pH test after 24 hours to insure safe canning was accomplished and the pH is below 4.5.

green tomato chutney

This is less sweet than the other chutneys you will encounter in this book. It is one of the reasons it is so popular. Used on pork, chicken and curry dishes, the southern heritage of the green tomato adds a little something special to this blend. A favorite way to serve as hors d'oeuvres is to mix a can of white chicken meat with $1/3$ to $1/2$ cup Green Tomato Chutney, 1 tablespoon mayonnaise, and 2 teaspoons curry powder. Mix and blend well. Serve on crackers or on Melba rounds.

CANNING NOTES
- **This is a hot pack, acidified recipe.**
- **Initial pH will be below 4.**
- **The recipe makes approximately 6 pint jars.**
- **The recipe can be doubled.**

INGREDIENTS
2 pounds green tomatoes, diced
2 pounds Granny Smith apples, peeled, cored and diced
$3/4$ pound onion, diced

2 lemons, sliced and seeded and slices halved
$1/2$ ounce garlic, diced fine
$1/2$ pound raisins
$1 1/2$ tablespoons mustard seed
$1/2$ tablespoon cayenne pepper
1 tablespoon ground ginger
$1/2$ tablespoon cinnamon

SOLUTION
2 cups cider vinegar
$1 1/2$ pounds brown sugar

Prepare ingredients. Place mixed solution in pot, add ingredients and bring to boil.

Reduce heat and cook down until thick, about 1 hour.

Conduct initial pH test. If pH is below 4.3, it is fine. To reduce, add vinegar 2 tablespoons at a time.

Hot pack above 190 degrees F according to the safe canning practices outlined on page 51.

Perform final pH testing after 24 hours to insure safe canning was accomplished and the pH is below 4.5.

green tomatoes

Commercially, tomatoes are picked green, so those that have already ripened on the vine are usually available for the asking. At farmers markets, I am continually asked, "Where does one find a green tomato?" Few seem to have heard of the variety. In fact, wherever they grow, tomatoes grow green. A green tomato is, simply, unripened. Andrea and Jack Limehouse, of Limehouse Produce, used to maintain a stock of three cases (seventy-five pounds) of green tomatoes each week. That was for the errant chef who might be trying something old, something new. Then came the movie, *Fried Green Tomatoes*. Today, that food distributor brings in one hundred thirty cases every day, year-round!

green tomato soup

This last green tomato recipe is different and unique. The finished product has some kick to it, but one can adjust the type and number of hot peppers accordingly—just don't cut them out entirely. Green Tomato Soup uses three ingredients that, for some, might offend the palate. The taste of capers dominates. Others find the heat of peppers too much to stand, even though it's just a little heat. The old guard in Charleston are wimps when it comes to spice. I was sampling my gumbo one Saturday when my mom's friend came to the booth. "Oh, Stevie," she said, "it's so hot." "It only has 1/16th of a teaspoon of cayenne per quart," I told her. "Well," she said, "I sure can taste it, " as she fanned her hand before her mouth while feigning a swoon. This soup would turn her insides out! Others are offended by the use of ham stock. If you can get through those hurdles, you are about to experience an epiphany in the world of soups. Nothing beats a hot bowl of soup on a cold winter day.

My favorite way to enjoy this soup is as a starter course for multi-course or formal dinners. Chill the jar and, because the soup is rich, reduce the individual portions by serving in small vessels like ramekins rather than soup bowls. Put a dollop of sour cream in the center of each little bowl. I add to the presentation by hanging three shrimp on each ramekin's edge—it makes a striking display. Regardless of what I prepare for a dinner party, and no matter how wonderful it is, when guests are leaving, they're still talking about the little first course. And it's out of a jar, no less!

CANNING NOTES
- **This is a hot pack, acidified recipe.**
- **Both initial and final pH will be at 4.**
- **The recipe makes 192 ounces or 6 quarts.**
- **The recipe can be doubled or halved.**

INGREDIENTS
2 pounds onions, rough chopped
$1/3$ pound jalapeños, deveined, seeded and chopped
3 ounces garlic cloves, minced
$3/4$ cup olive oil
20 bay leaves
9 pounds green tomatoes, cored and each cut into 6 wedges
3 quarts ham stock (low sodium is preferable)
1 cup capers
2 teaspoons salt
2 teaspoons coarse-ground pepper
$1/2$ cup lemon juice
2 teaspoons hot sauce

Saute onions, peppers and garlic in olive oil in a pot until onion is clear, about 10 minutes.

Put bay leaves in a small pot with 2 cups water and boil for 10 minutes. Strain liquid into pot with vegetables and discard leaves.

Add tomato wedges and ham stock to the pot, bring to a boil and reduce heat. Stirring often, cook just below boiling until tomatoes are very soft, about 30 minutes.

Remove all from pot and, in small batches, purée in a food processor or blender.

Return purée to pot, add capers, salt, pepper, lemon juice and hot sauce and bring to a low boil.

Conduct initial pH test. If pH is below 4.3, it is fine. To reduce, add lemon juice a tablespoon at a time.

Hot pack above 190 degrees F according to the safe canning practices outlined on page 51.

Perform final pH testing after 24 hours to insure safe canning was accomplished and the pH is below 4.5.

southern tomato sauce

There was a time when every family had its own recipe for tomato sauce. As Italian cooking gained popularity, the sauces moved from distinctly southern to more international. Palates are palates the world over and the folks in Italy have had an extra two thousand years to perfect their sauce. Like old school, new school, this recipe offers a little of both. It can be ladled over rice in the southern tradition and will work equally well over pasta. Mix in some already cooked and peeled Carolina shrimp and feast either way.

CANNING NOTES
- **This is a hot pack, acidified recipe.**
- **The pH will be around 4.**
- **The recipe makes approximately 6 quart jars.**
- **The recipe can be halved or doubled.**

INGREDIENTS
$^2/_3$ cup olive oil
2 (12-ounce) cans tomato paste
2 pounds sweet onions, chopped

4 ounces garlic cloves, chopped fine
10 pounds ripe tomatoes, cored, cut and squeezed
1 pound green bell pepper, diced
$^1/_2$ teaspoon citric acid
$^1/_4$ cup fresh oregano, packed tight
$^1/_2$ cup chopped fresh basil, packed tight
$^1/_4$ cup chopped fresh parsley, packed tight
$^1/_4$ cup chopped fresh fennel, packed tight
$1^1/_2$ tablespoons coarse-ground pepper
4 teaspoons salt

Cook oil, tomato paste, onions and garlic in a pot until onions are clear. Add balance of ingredients except herbs and bring to a strong boil. Add herbs and disperse well.

Conduct initial pH test. If pH is below 4.3, it is fine. To reduce, add $^1/_8$ teaspoon citric acid at a time.

Hot pack above 205 degrees F according to the safe canning practices outlined on page 51.

Perform final pH testing after 24 hours to insure safe canning was accomplished and the pH is below 4.5.

tomato salsa

Store-bought salsas come a dime a dozen. But it is not until one begins making one's own that you realize the difference between the commercially canned version and the real thing. It is just the nature of the commercial beast, and believe me, it is a monster. When we would sample our Pluff Mud, we did it as a chip dip that included salsa as an ingredient. We used the cheapest we could find. Still, our customers wanted to know the brand. It was Tom who finally said, "Dad, this is ridiculous; let's make our own." We did. Today, our salsa is right up there among the best-selling products we created.

CANNING NOTES
- **This is a hot pack, acidified recipe.**
- **The pH will be below 4.**
- **The recipe makes approximately 6 pint jars.**
- **The recipe can be doubled.**

INGREDIENTS
5 pounds very ripe tomatoes, squeezed then chopped

$1/2$ pound onion, diced
1 green bell pepper, diced
$2^1/2$ ounces garlic cloves, minced fine
$1^1/2$ ounces jalapeño peppers, diced
$1/3$ cup lime juice
2 tablespoons sugar
$1/2$ tablespoon salt
$1/2$ cup chopped cilantro, firmly packed

Prepare, measure and place in a pot all ingredients except cilantro. Bring to 190 degrees F.

Add cilantro just before canning, but before initial pH testing.

Conduct initial pH test. If pH is below 4.3, it is fine. To reduce, add lime or lemon juice 1 tablespoon at a time.

Hot pack above 185 degrees F according to the safe canning practices outlined on page 51.

Perform final pH testing after 24 hours to insure safe canning was accomplished and pH is below 4.5.

vine-ripe **red tomatoes**

Many vignettes have been written about the southern tomato. For the first half of the twentieth century these sun-sweetened red orbs were one of the Lowcountry's biggest crops. There is little in the food world that gives as much pleasure as a simple tomato sandwich, a single piece of white bread slathered with mayonnaise and a thick slice of bright red, just picked, beefsteak tomato plunked on top and sprinkled with salt and pepper. Many an afternoon I have pigged out on these sandwiches until there were sores around my lips from the tomato's acidity.

Growers were so plentiful that many had their own canneries to preserve the fine ripe fruit that couldn't go to market because of ripening or because, into the season, prices started falling as the markets flooded. Farmers took advantage of the vine-ripened fruits and processed them. Today, there are few growers and not a farm cannery remains. The following recipes require the freshest, ripest, field picked tomatoes one can find. A few call for peeled tomatoes. Just plunk the tomatoes in boiling water until a split appears on the skin, remove, dump in cool water and peel—the skin slides off easily.

gazpacho

Speaking about foreign shores and recipes, this chilled soup does as much for the southern tomato as a coronation does for a princess. Both deserve a throne of honor. Serve chilled as a first course or have as a light and fulfilling lunch.

CANNING NOTES
- **This is a hot pack, acidified recipe.**
- **Final pH will be below 4.1.**
- **The recipe makes 4 quarts.**
- **The recipe can be doubled.**

INGREDIENTS
5 pounds ripe tomatoes, peeled, seeded, and chopped (in a food processor)
4 cups tomato juice (like Campbell's, one without added ingredients)
1^1/$_2$ cups diced cucumbers (peeled)
1 cup diced green bell pepper
^{3}/$_4$ cup lemon juice
^{1}/$_2$ cup diced celery
^{1}/$_3$ cup chopped green onion
^{1}/$_3$ cup diced white onion
^{1}/$_4$ cup minced garlic cloves
2 tablespoons hot sauce (Tabasco or equivalent)
1 tablespoon sugar
1 tablespoon balsamic vinegar
1 tablespoon salt
2 teaspoons coarse-ground pepper

Prepare all ingredients and place in a pot. Over medium heat, bring to 195 degrees F.

Conduct initial pH test. If pH is below 4.3, it is fine. To reduce, add lemon juice 1 tablespoon at a time.

Hot pack at 195 degrees F according to the safe canning practices outlined on page 51.

Perform final pH testing after 24 hours to insure safe canning was accomplished and the pH is below 4.5.

red tomato chutney

Most chutneys are cooked down for inordinately long periods to render and concentrate the sugars from the fruits. Not so with the Red Tomato Chutney. Because it is brought to temperature and held for a far shorter period, the freshness of the ingredients gets canned right along with the flavors. Many use this as a substitute for ketchup. Traditionally, it is present when rice and roasts are on the table.

CANNING NOTES
- **This is a hot pack, acidified recipe.**
- **Final pH is under 4.**
- **The recipe makes 5 pints.**
- **The recipe can be doubled or halved.**

INGREDIENTS
4 pounds ripe tomatoes, cored and chopped
1¹/₄ cups sugar

1 green bell pepper, diced
1 cup raisins
1 cup currants
³/₄ cup diced yellow onion
¹/₄ cup shredded fresh ginger (peeled)
¹/₂ cup cider vinegar
¹/₂ cup lemon juice
2 tablespoons mustard seeds
1 tablespoon red pepper flakes

Prepare and place all ingredients in a pot. Bring to a low boil, and hold until chutney thickens, about 20 minutes; stir often.

Conduct initial pH test. If pH is below 4.3, it is fine. To reduce, add vinegar 1 tablespoon at a time.

Hot pack above 190 degrees F according to the safe canning practices outlined on page 51.

Perform final pH testing after 24 hours to insure safe canning was accomplished and pH is below 4.5.

tomato ketchup

It is so common an ingredient in our kitchens today, one has to wonder why anyone would take the time to make it. But, like mayonnaise, the real stuff is far different than what has become considered a standard. I leave it to the purest of hearts and masochists to task themselves with this chore. To twist Churchill's famous quote, never in the history of canning has so much gone into making so little.

CANNING NOTES
- **This is a hot pack, acidified recipe.**
- **pH will be below 4.**
- **The recipe makes approximately 5 half pints.**
- **The recipe can be doubled.**

INGREDIENTS
25 ripe tomatoes, peeled, cored, cut, squeezed, seeded, and chopped
$1^1/_2$ cups chopped yellow onion
2 large cloves garlic, diced

1 teaspoon whole cloves
2 cinnamon sticks
2 cups cider vinegar
1 cup sugar
$^1/_4$ cup lemon juice
2 teaspoons paprika
1 teaspoon powdered mustard
$^1/_2$ teaspoon allspice
$^1/_4$ teaspoon cayenne
$^1/_4$ teaspoon salt

Simmer tomatoes and onion in a pot until onion is clear, about 30 minutes.

Purée in a food processor or press through a sieve or strainer.

Return to the pot. At a slow boil, cook down by half, stirring often, about 1 to 2 hours.

While the tomato-onion purée is cooking, simmer garlic, cloves and cinnamon in a second pot with the vinegar for 30 minutes. Reserve the spiced vinegar and discard the solids.

Add to the pot with the tomato purée, the spiced vinegar and the remaining ingredients. Boil for 30 minutes, stirring frequently.

Conduct initial pH test. If pH is below 4.3, it is fine. To reduce, add more vinegar 1 tablespoon at a time.

Hot pack above 190 degrees F according to the safe canning practices outlined on page 51.

Perform final pH testing after 24 hours to insure safe canning was accomplished and the pH is below 4.5.

red tomato relish

Sometimes the sweetness of the red tomato just cannot be done without. Unfortunately, the lack of freshness and an overcooked taste has all but caused me to delete store bought ketchup from my condiment inventory. This is a ready substitute. Of course, it is wonderful on burgers, but also fine as an accompaniment to field peas, rice or on leftover roasts.

CANNING NOTES
- This is a hot pack, acidified recipe.
- pH will be below 4.
- The recipe makes approximately 7 pints.
- The recipe can be halved or doubled.

INGREDIENTS
6 pounds ripe tomatoes, peeled, cored, cut, squeezed and chopped
1^1/$_2$ pounds sweet onions, chopped

3 red bell peppers, diced
^{3}/$_4$ cup vinegar (5 percent acidity)
1 cup sugar
^{1}/$_2$ tablespoon salt
^{1}/$_2$ teaspoon ground cloves
^{1}/$_2$ teaspoon cinnamon
^{1}/$_2$ teaspoon allspice
^{1}/$_2$ teaspoon powdered ginger
^{1}/$_4$ teaspoon cayenne
^{1}/$_4$ teaspoon salt

Prepare and place all ingredients in a pot. Bring to a boil, reduce heat and cook for 45 minutes, stirring often.

Conduct initial pH test. If pH is below 4.3, it is fine. To reduce, add more vinegar 1 tablespoon at a time.

Hot pack above 195 degrees F according to the safe canning practices on page 51.

Perform final pH testing after 24 hours to insure safe canning was accomplished and the pH is below 4.5.

shrimp

As a boy with a boat, my challenge was earning money for gasoline. From age nine, I earned the right to play on the water by providing the family table with seafood. Many a meal was based upon the tide. I learned to catch crabs and fish and to throw a shrimp net. It took less than an hour to catch fifty crabs or harvest five pounds of creek shrimp. I still had plenty of time to play. When I was a little older and stronger I got a much heavier mullet net. Thursday night was always mullet stew and hush puppies. This was a simple time, a life of fields and crops, chickens and pigs, fish and shrimp. It was a life timed not by the clock but by the seasons and the tide.

In the pre-dawn, I would listen from my bed to the sounds: the roar of big diesels, the squeaking of blocks, and orders being shouted as the trawlers headed seaward, their decks and nets being readied. Six days a week, from 4 until 5 am, the parade moved down the river toward the sea. Near sunset, while my view was still blocked by a little island a half mile to the southwest, I could call out each boat's name just by the sight of the masthead and out riggers: *Bounty, Miss Frances, Dawn, Fawn, Curlew*. Seventy boats would return home each night to Adams Creek. Today, there are only two.

Shrimping continues. By mid-May, local shrimp boats have left their winter moorings on Lowcountry creeks and are once again trawling the inshore ocean waters off South Carolina. How much longer this colorful trade will remain is a question. U.S., Asian and Ecuadorian shrimp farming have all but fixed the price of shrimp while the costs of maintaining boats, buying fuel and paying crew continues to rise. The industry is, one boat at a time, vanishing.

The tragedy is not only of shrimpers and a dying fishery. In most coastal areas, the two great industries that shaped the landscape of our nation, small-scale farming and single boat fishing, are both almost gone. What does a country do when it no longer produces its own food? When it loses the skeleton of its cultural identity?

Charleston is a tourist destination and, as such, has a tourist-based economy. There are great and some even world-class restaurants. Enough so that in a week's visit or a month's stay, one never has to visit the same eating establishment twice. Yet, local shrimp are offered on only a few menus.

This is strange, considering our local shrimp once set the standard for the industry. Wild shrimp caught in these southern waters are a completely different animal with a completely different smell and flavor from farm-raised. When asked why so few local shrimp are served in local restaurants, excuses are diverse. Generally, the answers are price, uniform sizing, and continuity of access.

The fact is, the tourist doesn't know the difference, so why bother? Is this not tantamount to going to Kansas City and having a steak from Argentina? Still, there is a movement afoot. It began with a currently popular bumper sticker: Friends don't let friends eat foreign shrimp.

I give these next four recipes in honor of those watermen who leave their beds long before 4 am, work all day under a hot sun or in foul weather, only to return long after dark to receive a net token pittance for their effort.

pickled shrimp

Pickled Shrimp have a limited shelf life because the acidity of vinegar continues to slowly cook the shrimp just like the ceviche process for fish used in the tropics. Still, within their shelf life of six to eight months, these pickles remain delicious. Beyond the term they are still edible and tasty, but become rubbery. I often break open a jar to make a shrimp salad. The infused flavors add a delicious little extra touch to the salad used for sandwiches or on top of a bed of greens. For a shrimp salad, cut pickled shrimp into bite-sized chunks, add an equal amount of diced celery and half as much diced bell pepper (whichever color looks best for what you are doing). Add enough mayonnaise to the bowl to bind everything together and sprinkle with salt and pepper to suit.

CANNING NOTES
- This is a water bath, acidified recipe.
- pH is low. Final pH will be at or below 4.
- Recipe solution fills 6 pint jars or 12 half pints.
- One can make as many jars as practical.
- It takes 1 to 1$^1/_4$ pounds of raw shrimp to fill a pint jar.

IN EACH JAR
1 to 1$^1/_4$ pounds shrimp, cooked and peeled (see below)
1 white onion slice (a circular slice $^1/_4$ inch thick in bottom of jar)
2 teaspoons celery seed

1 teaspoon mustard seed
1 garlic clove (optional)
1 bay leaf
1 tablespoon olive oil

SOLUTION
3 cups white vinegar (5 percent acidity)
3 cups water
1 cup lemon juice
1 tablespoon salt
$^1/_2$ tablespoon celery seed
1 teaspoon turmeric

Put raw shrimp in boiling water. When first shrimp floats, shrimp are done.

Run shrimp under cold water to stop cooking; peel when cool.

Load jars with all ingredients except shrimp while solution is brought to a boil.

Pack shrimp tightly into jars because they will shrink. Add the boiling solution.

Conduct initial pH test on liquid from center jar before waterbathing. A level above 4.2 indicates improper acidity of vinegar. Discard solution and use correct vinegar.

Water bath to 183 degrees F according to the safe canning practices outlined on page 51.

Perform final pH testing after 24 hours by rinsing a shrimp in distilled water and then chopping or macerating in distilled water to insure safe canning was accomplished and the pH is below 4.5.

seafood cocktail sauce

Shrimp in the Lowcountry are right up there with rice and tomatoes. When shrimp are in, it is what we eat. This sauce, when mixed with cooked shrimp, will complement the seafood without overpowering the subtle, delicate flavors.

CANNING NOTES
- **This is a hot pack, acidified recipe.**
- **pH will be around 4.**
- **The recipe makes approximately 5 pints or 11 half pints.**
- **The recipe can be doubled or halved.**

INGREDIENTS
5 pounds tomatoes, cored, squeezed and diced
1 pound onions, diced
2 green bell peppers, diced
$1/2$ pound sugar
$1^1/2$ cups cider vinegar
2 tablespoons lemon juice

$1/2$ teaspoon ground cloves
2 teaspoons coarse-ground pepper
$1/2$ cup Tabasco
$1/2$ cup Worcestershire sauce
$1^1/2$ tablespoons minced garlic
$1/4$ pound fresh horseradish, grated fine
2 tablespoons paprika
2 teaspoons celery seed
$1^1/2$ teaspoons salt
$1^1/2$ tablespoons cornstarch (mixed with water to make a thick paste)
2 tablespoons chopped fresh basil, packed tight*
1 tablespoon ground oregano*
1 tablespoon picked thyme*

Combine all ingredients except cornstarch and fresh herbs in a pot.

Bring to a boil, reduce heat and cook for 1 hour, stirring frequently.

Add cornstarch mixture and continue to cook until mixture thickens. Add herbs and mix well.

Conduct initial pH test. If pH is below 4.3, it is fine. To reduce, add more lemon juice, 1 teaspoon at a time.

Hot pack above 190 degrees F according to the safe canning practices outlined on page 51.

Perform final pH testing after 24 hours to insure safe canning was accomplished and the pH is below 4.5.

***HINT:** Combine the herbs with a little of the vinegar in a blender for a finer chop.

charleston creole sauce

By describing my favorite way to prepare shrimp creole, one might think I was a heart surgeon attempting to cultivate new business. In a heavy sautéing skillet, fry two pieces of bacon until crisp. Remove the bacon and fold in a paper towel to cool. To the remnants in the pan (bacon grease and crackle), add the jar of creole, stirring and mixing well. At the first sign of boiling, reduce the heat, crumble and add the bacon and add 1^1/$_2$ pounds cooked and peeled wild-caught shrimp. Let the shrimp heat only, not cook! Serve over a shallow bed of rice.

CANNING NOTES
- **This is a water bath, acidified recipe.**
- **pH is low. Final pH will be below 4.**
- **The solution will fill 6 pint jars. Half pints are ineffective, but quarts work.**
- **One can make as many jars as is practical.**
- **Each jar will require approximately ^{1}/$_2$ pound artichokes.**

INGREDIENTS
^{1}/$_4$ **pound butter (1 stick)**
2 pounds onions, chopped
1 pound green bell peppers, diced
1^1/$_2$ ounces jalapeños, seeded and deveined
^{1}/$_2$ **bunch celery, diced**
4 cloves garlic, minced
1 (12-ounce) can tomato paste
7 pounds tomatoes, halved, squeezed and chopped
2^1/$_2$ tablespoons picked thyme, packed tight
^{1}/$_4$ **cup lemon juice**
4 bay leaves
2 teaspoons salt
1 teaspoon coarse-ground pepper
^{1}/$_2$ **teaspoon cayenne pepper**
^{1}/$_4$ **teaspoon paprika**

Melt butter in a pot. Add onions, peppers, celery, garlic and tomato paste and sauté until onion is clear, about 10 to 15 minutes.

Add balance of ingredients and bring to a low boil, stirring often.

Conduct initial pH test. If pH is below 4.3, it is fine. To reduce, add more lemon juice, 1 tablespoon at a time.

Hot pack at 205 degrees F according to the safe canning practices outlined on page 51.

Perform final pH testing after 24 hours to insure safe canning was accomplished and the pH is below 4.5.

charleston gumbo

I call this Charleston Gumbo, to distinguish it from the gumbos of Cajun heritage. Big difference! I have mentioned the Charlestonian palate's aversion to heat. Well, the Louisiana cousin to our gumbo is spicy hot and, instead of okra as a thickener, those folks with French, Spanish and American Indian influence use ground sassafras leaves called filé. Okra came to this country by way of the slaves from West Africa and the west African word for okra is gumbo. Our gumbo might not be as famous as Cajun gumbo, but it just might be more original.

Gumbo is one hundred percent southern and like so many southern dishes this one, too, is served over rice. While having a bowl with a friend on St. Simons Island, it dawned on me that I could make gumbo and I could make it better. The drafting counter was in full operation on Monday morning. Cookbooks and ingredients spread across fifty feet of counters. Seven tries later we had what we wanted without compromise. Our gumbo's popularity was immediate. Into the second year of the product, a young and recent bride approached our market booth. She asked if we would mind taking the gumbo off the table. "Please, just like for 10 minutes," she pleaded. It seems her husband had unexpectedly accompanied her that day. For the better part of a year she'd been serving gumbo for supper after telling him she had made it just for him. He enjoyed it so much that he pestered her to make it more and more often. What can I say? It is that good! Try taking a jar and adding a pound of wild, cooked and peeled shrimp plus a small lobster, shelled and cut into small bites. Serve over rice. It is a supper not soon forgotten.

I wrap the quart jars in duct tape to take on my long distance kayak adventures. If I catch a fish, it's fish gumbo; if not, I always carry a can or two of white chicken meat. While others are eating freeze-dried whatever, it's gourmet dining for this paddler. For other striking combinations try adding slices of andouille sausage or skin and then cut up a rotisserie chicken. The combinations are limitless, the enjoyment immeasurable.

- This is a hot pack, acidified recipe.
- Initial pH should be at 4.1.
- The recipe makes approximately 192 ounces or 6 quarts jars.
- The recipe can be doubled or halved.

INGREDIENTS

8 pounds ripe tomatoes, cored
$2^1/_2$ pounds okra, sliced
$1^1/_2$ pounds onions, diced
$^1/_2$ pound green bell peppers, diced
1 ounce garlic cloves, minced
1 tablespoon salt
4 tablespoons sugar
$1^1/_2$ tablespoons coarse-ground pepper
$^1/_4$ teaspoon cayenne pepper
$^1/_2$ cup lemon juice
$^1/_4$ teaspoon citric acid
4 bay leaves
1 cup water
$^2/_3$ cup butter, melted
$^1/_3$ cup flour
$^1/_8$ cup fresh thyme, packed tight
2 ounces fresh basil, stems removed, chopped
$^1/_2$ ounce fresh parsley, stems removed, chopped

Prepare and place in a pot all ingredients except 1 tomato, herbs, butter and flour. Cook at just below boil until mixture begins to thicken.

In a saucepan, boil the water with bay leaves for 10 minutes; remove bay leaves and discard; replenish water to original 1 cup measurement and add to pot.

Prepare a roux of flour and butter* and stir into pot just before herbs are added.

Finely chop the herbs with reserved tomato and add just before canning.

Conduct initial pH test. If pH is below 4.3, it is fine. To reduce, add more citric acid $^1/_8$ teaspoon at a time.

Hot pack at 205 degrees F according to the safe canning practices outlined on page 51.

Perform final pH testing after 24 hours to insure safe canning was accomplished and the pH is below 4.5.

*To make the roux, melt the butter in a small pot. When hot, slowly add the flour a little at a time. Beat with a whisk until well blended, with no lumps. Keep pan on heat and stir continuously, moving the mixture off the bottom until the first signs of browning (darkening). The roux is ready. Be careful! If it burns, throw the roux away and begin again.

Dilly Beans
7/25/06

dilled string beans

When I returned to the South after thirty years in the wilderness, I was introduced to a bizarre term, Dilly Beans. I had to wonder. This was nothing my grandmother ever did. Then a woman in the upstate gave me a sample and I knew that one day I'd produce this delicious salad ingredient with so many other uses—like as a party finger food served chilled on a platter right out of the jar. There are drinking establishments in Charleston that actually buy these pickled beans, cases at a time, for serving in martinis in lieu of olives. The Dilly Bean Martini is a local favorite. The Dirty Dilly Martini is one where a dash of the pickling liquid is added along with the vermouth.

CANNING NOTES
- **This is a water bath, acidified recipe.**
- **pH is low. Final pH will be below 4.**
- **The solution will fill 7 pint jars.**
- **One can make as many jars as is practical.**
- **Each jar will require $^3/_4$ pound of fresh, good-quality string beans.**

IN EACH JAR
$^3/_4$ **pound string beans, trimmed to canning jar length (4$^1/_4$ inches)**
2 cloves garlic
$^1/_2$ **teaspoon dill seed**
$^1/_4$ **teaspoon whole mustard seeds**
1 hot chili pepper, fresh or dried (optional)

SOLUTION
5 cups white vinegar (5 percent acidity)
5 cups water
$^1/_2$ **cup salt**
3$^1/_2$ teaspoons red pepper flakes
$^1/_2$ **tablespoon celery seed**
1 teaspoon turmeric

Wash beans and trim from stem end to 4$^1/_4$ inches (to fit in jar), discarding stem end.

Put garlic, dill and mustard seeds in jars, then tightly pack in beans.

Insert chili pepper so it is visible on one side of the jar.

Bring solution to a strong boil and then fill jars in canning rack with solution.

Conduct initial pH test on liquid in center jar. If pH is above 4.2, vinegar with incorrect acidity was used, or, the solution of water and vinegar was improperly measured. Discard liquid and begin again.

Water bath to 185 degrees F according to the safe canning practices outlined on page 51.

Perform final pH testing after 24 hours by rinsing one bean in distilled water and either macerate in a blender or chop and crush bean in 1 cup of distilled water before testing to insure safe canning was accomplished and the pH is below 4.5.

blackberry preserves

The blackberry harvest begins in early June and runs through July. No summer month gets by without a new preserve. June is blackberries. By the month's end they have sweetened sufficiently to make excellent preserves. I am frequently asked if I have removed the seeds. I don't; it is part of the fruit and too many of the flavors are dependent upon them. For those that don't like the texture, I suggest skipping to the July Blueberry Preserves on page 132.

CANNING NOTES
- **This is a hot pack, acid recipe.**
- **pH is not an issue. No testing is required.**
- **The recipe makes 8 pint jars or 16 half pints.**
- **The recipe can be halved but not doubled. If reduced, combine steps 3 and 4.**

10 cups blackberries, lightly rinsed and stems removed
2 packs pectin or $^2/_3$ cup bulk pectin
14 cups sugar

Prepare and place all ingredients except sugar in a pot.

Over a high heat, bring to a strong boil.

Add half the sugar and, stirring frequently, bring to a partial boil. Add balance of sugar and bring to a strong, rolling boil.

Begin a 3-minute countdown to canning; after 2 minutes, check for signs of jelling.

Hot pack according to the safe canning practices outlined on page 51.

july

THE JULY HARVEST is substantial and equal to June's, although by late July only the heartiest of fruits and vegetables can survive the harsh summer sun. There remains canning opportunity o' plenty. If there were another word in South Carolina for the month named for Julius Caesar, it would be Peachy. Georgia calls itself the Peach State, but it is a fact that South Carolina's crop exceeds Georgia's.

peach mint preserves

The flavor of mint with peach is most refreshing. Mint always reminds me of cool afternoon breezes, and peaches the heart of summer. I can just picture my forefathers on a porch overlooking oaks, rivers and marshes, enjoying a frosty mint julep and a bowl of creamy, homemade vanilla ice cream topped with these preserves. Back then, they would make this a daily summer afternoon ritual.

CANNING NOTES
- **This is a hot pack, acid recipe.**
- **pH is not an issue. No testing is required.**
- **The recipe makes 6 half pint jars.**
- **The recipe can be halved or doubled.**

INGREDIENTS
4 cups diced peaches (peeled)
$1/2$ cup chopped mint, packed tight
2 tablespoons lemon juice
1 pack pectin or $1/3$ cup bulk pectin
$5^1/2$ cups sugar

Prepare and place all ingredients except the sugar in a pot.

Over a high heat, stirring often, bring to a strong boil. Add the sugar and, stirring frequently, bring to a rolling boil. Begin the $1^1/2$-minute timing before canning; but after 1 minute, check for signs of jelling.

Hot pack according to the safe canning practices outlined on page 51.

peach preserves

There are many uses for our wonderful peaches, but every pantry needs a few of the basics. Here's the plain and simple. Fresh peach preserves are so different from their commercial counterpart that one might want to make the run early so several more can be made later.

CANNING NOTES

- This is a hot pack, acid recipe.
- pH is not an issue. No testing is required.
- The recipe makes 6 pint jars or 12 half pints.
- The recipe can be halved but not doubled. If reduced, combine steps 3 and 4.

INGREDIENTS

8 cups diced peaches (peeled)
$1/4$ cup lemon juice
2 packs pectin or $2/3$ cup bulk pectin
11 cups sugar

Prepare and place all ingredients except sugar in a pot.

Over high heat, bring to a strong boil. Add half the sugar and return to the beginning of a boil, stirring frequently. Add balance of sugar and bring to a rolling boil.

Begin a 3-minute timing before canning; at 2 minutes, check for signs of jelling.

Hot pack according to the safe canning practices outlined on page 51.

VARIATION: PEACH CINNAMON PRESERVES

Made in the fashion of the Strawberry Cinnamon Preserves (see page 73) in the March section, for each jar to be produced, add to the standard peach preserve recipe cinnamon sticks—1 per jar. Remove the sticks during the timing phase and place in jars.

peaches

The first varieties of these succulent fruits are picked in mid June, but it takes the hot summer sun to really sweeten the meat. There are literally hundreds of varieties of this plant of the rose family, but a major and significant distinction, as far as canning goes, is between the freestone and the clingstone. With the first, the pit or seed is easily plucked from the halved peach, whereas the other clings for dear life to the surrounding body. It is labor and time, one of which you already have plenty and the other, not enough. Avoid all clingstone varieties. Peaches must be picked ripe to peel easily. As with all fruits, the riper before picking the better the flavor. But in the case of peaches, the fuzzy skin, which must be removed, peels well only on ripe-picked fruit. Dunk the individual peaches in boiling water for 1 to 2 minutes, remove and dash them into very cold water until cool. If picked very ripe but still firm, the skins will slough off, leaving a smooth, shiny unblemished surface. This will be most important later.

peach salsa

For two years, folks at farmers markets pressed us to create a peach salsa. We continued to resist because we could not find a uniqueness. We struggled with a few attempts, but the efforts, although okay, were not the earth shattering results that we demanded for a new product. Then one day, dreaming out of the box, I saw the ingredient that would make peach salsa exactly what this father and son team requires. We went to work. The ingredient was mint and, as they say, the rest is history. Serve it like any salsa with chips or ladle over white fish like grouper or flounder the last 5 minutes of cooking.

CANNING NOTES
- **This is a hot pack, acidified recipe.**
- **The pH will be around 4.**
- **The recipe makes approximately 10 pints.**
- **The recipe can be doubled or halved.**

INGREDIENTS

5 pounds very ripe tomatoes, squeezed then chopped
5 pounds peaches, peeled and chopped
3 pounds onions, diced
2 green bell peppers, diced
2 ounces jalapeño peppers, diced (do not seed or devein)
2 tablespoons sugar
1 tablespoon powdered ginger
2 teaspoons red pepper flakes
2 teaspoons salt
1/2 cup chopped cilantro, with stems
1/2 cup chopped mint
1/2 cup lime juice
1/2 cup peach cider or peach nectar

Prepare and place all ingredients in a pot except cilantro, mint, lime juice and peach cider in a pot.

Bring ingredients to just below boiling; add reserved ingredients.

Conduct initial pH test. If pH is below 4.3, it is fine. To reduce, add lime juice, 1 tablespoon at a time.

Hot pack at 190 degrees F according to the safe canning practices outlined on page 51.

Perform initial pH testing after 24 hours to insure safe canning was accomplished and the pH is below 4.5.

peach chutney

This is by far the most popular of the eight chutneys we make, selling three to one over any of the others. It's not that the others are not good—they're great—but our peach is the sweetest. After you break the seal on a jar, as long as you keep the lid on and the chutney refrigerated it will keep for longer than it takes to use it. For quick hors d'oeuvres, actually the fastest hors d'oeuvres in the South, just pour some peach chutney over a block of cream cheese and serve with water crackers. Place some in a condiment bowl when serving chicken, pork or any curry dish. My favorite usage is with pork tenderloins. Prepare the meat as you normally would for cooking. While roasting in the oven, when the pork is half done, or on the grill just after the tenderloin has been turned, make a $1/2$- to 1-inch-deep incision the length of the tenderloin and fill it with peach chutney. Continue to cook until done (internal temperature 170 degrees F). Allow the meat to cool for 5 to 10 minutes; cut into medallions and serve with a tablespoon of chutney on the side. Here's a little secret. Always make sure a few medallions make it to the "frig." On toast with mayonnaise, salt and pepper, the pork sandwich with the peach flavor permeated throughout is right up there with June's tomato sandwiches.

CANNING NOTES

- **This is a hot pack, acid recipe.**
- **pH is not an issue. No testing is required.**
- **The recipe makes 10 or more pints or 21 half pints.**
- **The recipe can be halved or doubled.**

INGREDIENTS

10 pounds peaches, peeled, pitted and diced
$1/4$ cup mustard seed
$1/4$ cup red pepper flakes
$3^1/2$ pounds sugar
1 pint white vinegar (5 percent acidity)
$1/4$ pound crystallized ginger
2 tablespoons minced garlic
$3/4$ pound raisins

Prepare and place all ingredients in a pot.

Cook down on a low boil until thick, raisins float and temperature goes above 212 degrees F (all water is cooked out). Do not cook beyond this point.

Hot pack above 195 degrees F according to the safe canning practices outlined on page 51.

garden vegetable soup

On the sharply angled corner of Broad and Savage Streets in Charleston is a family grocery that has bucked the trends of time. Against giant supermarkets, this tiny store has been serving faithful customers since the end of World War II. Each day, Robert Burbage and his sons produce a fresh version of this soup. It is from them that I got the idea and I thank them.

This medley of vegetables can often be found in a backyard or a "back forty" garden. In reality, not all the ingredients are timely and ready for the pot in the same season, so you have to be the judge as to when to make the soup. It can be a soup or, by adding rice and either chicken, fish or meat, it can become a whole supper. I often make a complete meal for four by adding 2 cups cooked rice and 1 pound diced meat, seafood or poultry to the contents. Simple and nutritious, GVS, as we called it in the office, is one of those staples that finds its way onto my kayak camping menu. When it comes to having a bowl of soup, there are few recipes that will taste this fresh. Part of the reason for the freshness is the careful monitoring of temperature before canning: too hot and one loses the fresh garden taste, but just one or two degrees under the required canning temperature and lids will buckle from growing bacteria.

CANNING NOTES
- **This is a hot pack, acidified recipe.**
- **The pH should be below 4.2.**
- **The recipe makes 192 ounces or 6 quarts.**
- **The recipe can be doubled or halved.**

INGREDIENTS
7 pounds ripe tomatoes, diced
1¹/₂ pounds okra, sliced
1¹/₂ pounds onion, diced
1¹/₂ pounds baby lima beans
1 quart beef stock (or try using a vegetarian version)
3 tablespoons extra virgin olive oil
1 tablespoon coarse-ground pepper
¹/₂ tablespoon salt
¹/₃ cup lemon juice
¹/₃ cup sugar
¹/₂ teaspoon citric acid
¹/₄ cup fresh basil, packed tight
2 tablespoons fresh thyme, stems removed, packed tight
5 ears corn, cut off the cob

Prepare and place all ingredients except basil, thyme and corn in a pot.

Bring soup to a low boil. Add remaining ingredients and return to a low boil.

Check initial pH test. If pH is below 4.2, it is fine. To reduce, add 1 tablespoon of lemon juice and ¹/₈ teaspoon citric acid at a time.

Hot pack above 205 degrees F according to the safe canning practices outlined on page 51.

Perform final pH testing after 24 hours to insure safe canning was accomplished and the pH is below 4.5.

pepper relish or hot pepper relish

July is dead center into the pepper season, both sweet and hot. This old time favorite is full of flavor and is served with meats, fish or vegetables and with rice. For the sweet peppers, use green, red, yellow or a combination.

CANNING NOTES
- **This is a hot pack, acidified recipe.**
- **Both initial and final pH will be below 4.1.**
- **The recipe makes 4 pints or 8 half pints.**
- **The recipe can be doubled or halved.**

INGREDIENTS
6 bell peppers, red, green, yellow or any combination, diced

1 pound yellow onions, diced large
2 jalapeño peppers, diced (for Hot Pepper Relish only)
$^3/_4$ cup white vinegar (5 percent acidity)
1 cup sugar
$^1/_2$ tablespoon salt
$^1/_2$ tablespoon mustard seed

Prepare and place all ingredients in a pot.

Bring to a boil, reduce and cook for 30 minutes to 1 hour, or until free liquid is gone.

Conduct initial pH test. If pH is 4.3 or below, it is fine. To reduce, add 2 tablespoons vinegar at a time.

Hot pack above 205 degrees F according to the safe canning practices outlined on page 51.

Perform final pH testing after 24 hours to insure safe canning was accomplished and the pH is below 4.5.

fruit chutney

Traditionally, chutneys are heavy affairs with long cook down times to render the sugars from the fruits and vegetables. This chutney is different. It is light, with subtle flavors, gentle like a summer breeze and is a fine accompaniment to servings of fresh fish and chicken. The multiple bright colors add to the chutney's mystique.

CANNING NOTES

- **This is a water bath, acidified recipe.**
- **pH is low. Final pH will be below 4.**
- **The chutney will fill 6 pint jars.**
- **This recipe can be doubled.**
- **All produce measurements are stated in prepared weights.**

INGREDIENTS

$1^1/_4$ pounds papaya, diced
1 pound mango, seeded and diced
$^3/_4$ pound fresh pineapple, prepared and diced
$^3/_4$ pound Red Delicious apples, cored and diced
$^3/_4$ pound pears, peeled and diced

$^1/_2$ pound red onion, chopped
$^1/_2$ pound red bell peppers, diced
$^1/_2$ pound green bell peppers, diced
$^1/_2$ pound yellow bell peppers, diced
$^1/_2$ pound dark raisins
$^1/_2$ pound light raisins
3 jalapeño peppers, sliced widthwise
3 cups cider vinegar
6 cups sugar
2 tablespoons turmeric
1 tablespoon ground cloves
1 stick cinnamon per canning jar
$^1/_2$ tablespoon celery seed
1 teaspoon turmeric

Prepare and place all ingredients except cinnamon sticks in a pot. Stirring often, bring to 170 degrees F.

Conduct initial pH test. If pH is below 4.3, it is fine. If above, improper acidity of vinegar was used. To reduce, add citric acid, a pinch at a time.

Put a cinnamon stick in each jar and then fill with chutney.

Water bath to 185 degrees F according to the safe canning practices outlined on page 51.

Perform final pH testing after 24 hours to insure safe canning was accomplished and the pH is below 4.5.

Hot Pepper Jelly
7/21/06

hot pepper jelly

This is typical me. I put off making this over cream cheese hors d'oeuvres ingredient because it was not from the Old South. What I failed to see was that neither were my customers. Now, literally at every market, this jelly is the star, selling three against one to any other product I produce.

CANNING NOTES

- **This is a hot pack, sugar saturated recipe.**
- **pH is not an issue. No testing is required.**
- **This recipe makes 6 half pints.**
- **The recipe can be doubled but not halved.**

INGREDIENTS

1 cup small dice green bell pepper (seeded)
1 cup small dice red bell pepper (seeded)
$1/2$ cup chopped fine jalapeño peppers (seeded)

$1^1/2$ cups cider vinegar
$6^1/2$ cups sugar
$1/2$ tablespoon butter
1 tablespoon red pepper flakes
1 pack liquid pectin (Certo)

Bring all ingredients except pectin to a rolling boil. Add pectin and return to a boil.

Time for $1^1/2$ minutes and take off burner.

Hot pack according to the safe canning practices outlined on page 51.

garlic pepper jelly

The popularity of garlic continues to increase. It is no wonder. The longest lived people seem to be some of the heaviest garlic eaters. Garlic cloves are thought to lower cholesterol and reduce blood pressure, just to name a few benefits. Heavy garlic eaters repel bugs, and even heavier consumers, people. Like my pickled garlic, this recipe will not affect one's breath but it will positively affect one's popularity when it is served over cream cheese at a party. And, for a special treat, try coating lamb chops or pork chops with this jelly as they come off the grill or out of the broiler.

CANNING NOTES
- **This is a hot pack, sugar saturated recipe.**
- **pH is not an issue. No testing is required.**
- **This recipe makes 6 half pints.**
- **The recipe can be doubled, but not halved.**

INGREDIENTS
$3/4$ cup small dice green bell pepper (seeded)
$3/4$ cup small dice red bell pepper (seeded)
$1/3$ cup jalapeño pepper, seeded and chopped fine

$1/2$ cup minced garlic
$1 1/2$ cups cider vinegar
$6 1/2$ cups sugar
$1/2$ tablespoon butter
1 tablespoons red pepper flakes
1 pack liquid pectin (Certo)

Bring all ingredients except pectin to a rolling boil. Add pectin and return to boil.

Time for $1 1/2$ minutes and check for jelling; continue until ready.

Hot pack according to the safe canning practices outlined on page 51.

blueberry preserves

By the beginning of July the crop that began a month ago has matured to an unbelievable sweetness. This is the time to make preserves and blueberry marmalade. No respectable pantry should be without jars of each.

CANNING NOTES
- **This is a hot pack, acid recipe.**
- **pH is not an issue. No testing is required.**
- **The recipe makes 6 pints or 12 half pints.**
- **The recipe can be halved but not doubled. If halved, add all the sugar at once.**

INGREDIENTS
8 cups blueberries, rinsed and stems removed
$1/4$ cup lemon juice
1 tablespoon butter
2 packs pectin or $2/3$ cup bulk pectin
8 cups sugar

Prepare and place all ingredients except the sugar in a pot.

Over a medium-high heat, bring to a strong boil. Add half the sugar and, stirring frequently, bring to a partial boil. Add balance of sugar and bring to a strong, rolling boil.

Begin a 2-minute count down; after 1 minute, check for signs of jelling.

Hot pack according to the safe canning practices on page 51.

blueberry marmalade

No matter how many different preserves I stock in the pantry, I always run out of my marmalades first. Blueberry is no exception. It is the sweet and sour combination on the palate that draws morning southern biscuit eaters to the marmalade pot like flies to light. The deep dark blue of the preserve accented with the yellows and oranges of the rind give a most attractive presentation even on a formal breakfast table.

CANNING NOTES
- **This is a hot pack, acid recipe.**
- **pH is not an issue. No testing is required.**
- **This recipe makes 6 pints or 13 half pints.**
- **The recipe can be halved but not doubled. If halved, add all the sugar at once.**

INGREDIENTS
5 cups blueberries, rinsed and stems removed
3 thin-skinned oranges, thin sliced, seeded and quartered
2 lemons, thin sliced, seeded and quartered
1 cup water
$^1/_2$ tablespoon butter
2 packs pectin or $^2/_3$ cups bulk pectin
11 cups sugar

Prepare and place all ingredients in a pot except the sugar.

Over high heat, stirring often, bring to a rolling boil. Add half the sugar, mix well and stir until ingredients show signs of boiling. Add balance of sugar and bring to a full, rolling boil.

Stirring continuously, time rolling boil for up to 3 minutes.

Take pot off heat and hot pack by ladling marmalade into sterilized jars according to the safe canning practices on page 51.

NOTE 1: Blueberries have lots of natural pectin, so jelling comes faster than with other fruits. After the first minute of timing, begin testing for jelling.

NOTE 2: Stir the ingredients well as you ladle into jars so each jar gets a portion of whole fruit. Once in the jars, the chunks of fruit float to the top. After the 2-minute inverted requirement, right the jars and over the next 30 minutes or so, periodically check. Shake the jars to disperse the particulates uniformly until jelling sets the fruit.

august

THE DOLDRUMS OF SUMMER have arrived. Figs, so unique and delicate, are one of the special joys of August. By mid month, both the purple and yellow varieties are ready for processing. With temperatures sometimes over a hundred degrees F and the humidity over ninety percent, the land quietly cooks and just thinking of canning makes you hot. I remember my grandmother in her later years being helped to a chair for a break in a stifling kitchen where she toiled putting up jars for winter. At our canning plant, during those hot August days with ten 30,000-BTU burners going and a steam-jacketed kettle running, our testing thermometers often registered 125 degrees F while sitting on the shelf. We had to chuckle as we closed up shop, commenting on how cool the outdoor 100 degrees F felt. Everything is relative. Today, with air conditioning, any day can be a 75-degree joy, so there's no excuse except one's personal contribution against global warming. In that case, enjoy the heat and know that your pores will be cleaner than your neighbors.

colonial charleston chutney

The sea captains from far eastern ports brought recipes to the early Charleston colonists. Although local fruits and vegetables were often substituted for the exotic ingredients called for, this early chutney still uses spices that were arriving from Jamaica with the slave trade. The chutney is rich and different. I like to serve it as a side to rich meats.

CANNING NOTES
- **This is a hot pack, acidified recipe.**
- **The pH will be below 4.**
- **The recipe makes approximately 5 pint jars.**
- **The recipe can be doubled.**

INGREDIENTS
3 pounds ripe tomatoes, cored, halved and lightly squeezed
1 green bell pepper, diced

3 pounds peaches, skinned and chopped
1 small yellow onion, diced
$^1/_2$ cup raisins
$^1/_4$ pound crystallized ginger, chopped fine
$^3/_4$ pound brown sugar
1 teaspoon salt
1 cup cider vinegar
$1^1/_2$ tablespoons mustard seed
1 tablespoon allspice
1 teaspoon nutmeg

Prepare and place all ingredients in a pot. Cook at a low boil, stirring often, until mixture begins to thicken.

Conduct initial pH test. If pH is below 4.2, it is fine. To reduce, add more cider vinegar 2 tablespoons at a time.

Hot pack above 190 degrees F according to the safe canning practices on page 51.

Perform final pH testing after 24 hours to insure safe canning was accomplished and the pH is below 4.5.

whole fig preserves and jam

Figs come in two basic varieties: purple and yellow—the purple being more delicate. The yellow or brown—or those locally referred to as Turkey figs—are hearty when it comes to putting heat to them. Consequently, they make excellent whole fig preserves. There are two schools: whole figs and jam. They will never come together. Many find that with so many spreads available, the whole fig is a refreshing change. If not, or if one does not choose to balance a round fig on morning toast, a fig jam recipe follows. I make both. I use both. Whole Fig Preserves with a little syrup is especially good on vanilla ice cream.

FIG PRESERVES

CANNING NOTES
- **This is a hot pack, acid recipe.**
- **pH is not an issue. No testing is required.**
- **This recipe makes 6 half pint jars.**
- **The recipe can be doubled.**

FOR THE SOAK
2 tablespoons pickling lime
$1/2$ gallon water

FOR THE PRESERVES
3 pounds figs (with stems on)
2 pounds sugar

Soak figs covered in lime solution for 1 hour and then rinse well, twice.

Put figs and sugar in a pot and bring to a low, slow boil. The juices in the figs will form a syrup in the pot. Boil for at least 1 hour.

When figs are tender and cooked through, hot pack by gently ladling into jars and fill with boiling liquid according to the safe canning practices outlined on page 51.

FIG JAM

CANNING NOTES
- **This is a hot pack, acid recipe.**
- **pH is not an issue. No testing is required.**
- **This recipe makes 8 half pint jars.**
- **The recipe can be doubled, but sugar must be added in two equal increments, bringing figs to a low boil in between.**

INGREDIENTS
5 cups figs, crushed or chopped ($3 1/4$ pounds picked fruit)
$1/2$ cup lemon juice
$1/2$ cup water
$1/2$ tablespoon butter
1 pack pectin or $1/3$ cup bulk pectin
$7 1/2$ cups sugar

Prepare and place all ingredients except sugar in a pot.

Bring to a strong boil, stirring often. Add sugar and bring to a strong boil.

Stirring continuously, time for 1 minute, checking often for signs of jelling.

Hot pack according to the safe canning practices outlined on page 51.

okra pickles

Many southerners have been the butt of jokes because they eat the slimy stuff called okra. First brought to this country by slaves from Africa, okra has remained a popular, and even cherished, vegetable. The pods require a goodly dose of acidification to safely pickle. Still, the end result is something to behold. Pickled okra is not the slimy thing the steamed version becomes. They are firm, with a fine pickled flavor, go well in salads and are sought after as a party finger food. Pickled okra often arrives with the tailgate crowd at southern college football games. One will see "them good ol' boys" with a beer in one hand and a pickled okra pod in the other.

CANNING NOTES
- **This is a water bath, acidified recipe.**
- **pH of okra is high. Final pH will be around 4.1.**
- **The solution will fill 6 pint jars. Half pints will work, but only with small pods.**
- **One can produce as many jars as is practical.**
- **Each pint jar will require approximately $^3/_4$ pound of fresh okra.**

IN EACH JAR
$^3/_4$ **pound okra, washed and prepared**
2 cloves garlic
1 teaspoon mustard seeds
1 or 2 hot peppers (preferably red, like chili peppers)

BOILING SOLUTION
4 cups white vinegar (5 percent acidity)
2 cups water
6 tablespoons salt

Wash okra and trim any excess stems.

Put garlic and mustard seeds in jars and then fill the bottom with okra pointing up. Next, place a second layer of okra pointing down above and between the first layer. Be certain not to have okra ends sticking above the canning line on the jar.

Put peppers in last, pressed against the side of the jar half way down.

Place jars in canning rack and fill with boiling solution.

Conduct initial pH test of liquid in center jar. If above 4.2, either incorrect acidity vinegar was used or mixture of vinegar and water was improperly measured. Discard liquid and begin again.

Water bath to 185 degrees F according to the safe canning practices outlined on page 51.

Perform final pH testing after 24 hours by macerating an okra pod in 1 cup of distilled water to insure safe canning was accomplished and the pH is below 4.5.

NOTE: Okra is hollow and will absorb the majority of the canning liquid. This is fine, and I think looks better, although federal inspectors used to have a hissy fit with me when I did mine like this. They preferred that I keep topping off the liquid in the water bath jars as they heated. This is not necessary.

there's hot and
then there's hot sauce

I put off making a hot sauce for far too long. The little bottles have attained cult status and yet most are just hot. Let's face it: the primary ingredients are peppers and vinegar. How does one improve on that mixture? It was those cult groupies at our open-air markets and their macho husbands trying to show how hot they could take it that got me thinking. I finally gave in. I was tired of these tough guys sauntering up to the table, and, like a cowpoke from old television, invariably asking, "What's the hottest thing ya got, partner!" I had given my sensitive, heat averse, Charleston palate speech, for the last time.

The following month, with the debut of a hot sauce, was unforgettable. There was no choice but to name it, There's Hot and Then There's Hot Sauce. Unlike most of these concoctions, this one is filled with a bouquet of separate flavors and can be made even more flavorful by substituting Scotch Bonnets for the recipe's called for habañeros. I selected the latter simply because the South-of-the-Border pepper is easier to locate than its Jamaican cousin. A tiny dribble of this sauce adds wonders to many a meal from morning eggs to evening meats and rice. Just be cautious and add tiny bits at a time. Like salt, it is far easier to add more than to take back even the slightest pinch.

CANNING NOTES
- **This is a hot pack, acidified recipe.**
- **The pH will be below 4.**
- **The recipe makes approximately 6 or more half pints.**
- **The recipe can be doubled.**

INGREDIENTS
3/4 tablespoon minced garlic
1 small yellow onion, minced
2 tablespoons olive oil
1 pound fresh habañero peppers, chopped fine

1 1/2 pounds mangoes, peeled, seeded and diced (initial weight)
2 oranges, peeled, seeded, plugged and membranes removed
1/2 cup frozen orange juice concentrate
1 cup tomato purée
1 tablespoon lime juice
3/4 pound sugar
1/4 cup white vinegar (5 percent acidity)
3/4 teaspoon allspice
1/4 teaspoon salt

Saute garlic and onion in the oil until onion is clear. Combine all ingredients in a pot and bring to a boil.

Pour ingredients into a blender and blend until smooth.

Return purée to pot and bring to 205 degrees F.

Conduct initial pH test. If pH is below 4.3 is fine. To reduce, add more vinegar 1 tablespoon at a time.

Hot pack at above 200 degrees F according to the safe canning practices outlined on page 51.

Perform final pH testing after 24 hours to insure safe canning was accomplished and the pH is below 4.5.

pickled peaches

Near the end of the peach season comes a small variety of the fruit with a deep red skin. I like to use these because the red juices darken the syrup, in time, to a rich mahogany. The yellow orbs inside the colorful syrup make a sight to behold and give the presentation an equal to the taste of the product. These quart jars make cherished gifts. In the Old South many a Thanksgiving turkey and Christmas ham was surrounded by spiced peaches and often the syrup was used as a glaze, painted on during the last 30 minutes of cooking the bird or ham.

CANNING NOTES
- **This is a hot pack, acid recipe.**
- **pH is not an issue. No testing is required.**
- **This recipe makes 4 quart jars.**
- **The recipe can be adjusted to make as many jars as desired.**
- **40 to 50 small peaches should be picked or purchased to make the 4 jars.**

IN EACH JAR
1 cinnamon stick
2 or 3 ginger slices, fresh, skinned and sliced cross sectionally
9 to 11 peaches packed up to canning line, smooth peeled and with a clove stuck deep into each peach

BOILING SOLUTION
$1/2$ gallon cider vinegar
9 pounds sugar

Dunk peaches in boiling water for 1 to 3 minutes until skins are ready to slough off.

Dump peaches into iced water and, when cool, gently peel. (The smoother the body of the peeled peach, the better looking the finished product.)

Place peeled peaches into boiling solution until they begin to turn soft. A foaming boil will develop as the water cooks out of the fruit. Lower the temperature slightly. Stir carefully, as peaches can get damaged.

Pack fruit into jars and fill with hot syrup (insure liquid covers topmost peaches) and hot pack according to the safe canning practices on page 51.

peach leather

The oldest recipes from Charleston are recorded in *The Carolina Housewife*, the 1847 cookbook published anonymously at the time by a grand lady of the town, Sarah Rutledge, granddaughter to a signer of the Declaration of Independence. Peach Leather is not a preserve, nor is it a pickle, nor is it canned. But I include it here because this unusual delicacy is the great-great-great-etc. grandfather of fruit roll-ups. Originally, the spread was dried in the hot summer sun, cut, rolled and put away for children as a treat or reward for when they were good.

INGREDIENTS
2 pounds peaches, peeled, pitted and puréed
3 cups sugar
2 tablespoons lemon juice

Prepare the peaches. Peel, pit, purée and place in a pot.

Add sugar and lemon juice. Over medium heat, stirring often, bring to a boil.

Pour thin layers of peach purée onto large, nonstick shallow pans. Tilt pans to move purée around until thin—but not too thin—and evenly dispersed.

Place sheets in lowest temperature oven.

When no longer wet to touch but not crisp-dry (i.e. like the texture of leather), remove and allow to cool. Peel from pan.

On a cutting board, cut into rectangles, $2^1/2$ x 3 inches. Roll into short side. If removed before too dry, the rolls will stay together.

Roll Peach Leather rolls in sugar and store in an air-tight jar, ziplock bag or wrap in plastic wrap.

watermelon rind pickles

One cannot have a southern canning book without including the fruit most associated with the south—the watermelon. But pickling the rind is as much a northern delicacy as it is a southern labor of love. When going through my grandmother's recipes I found a letter from my paternal grandmother, a Yankee from Philadelphia. After my parents wedding, she sent the recipe for the pickle since there seemed to be a void in the Rockland Plantation repertoire of goodies.

CANNING NOTES
- **This is a hot pack, sugar saturated recipe.**
- **pH is not an issue. No testing is required.**
- **The recipe makes approximately 10 pints or 20 half pints.**
- **One can make as many jars as they have melons. Adjust liquid accordingly.**

INGREDIENTS
1 watermelon rind, prepared (see below)
$1/2$ cup canning lime
8 cups cider vinegar
8 pounds sugar
2 tablespoons whole allspice, tied in cheesecloth
2 tablespoons whole cloves, tied in same cheesecloth with allspice
1 stick cinnamon per pint jar ($1/2$ stick for $1/2$ pints)

Peel the dark green off the melon and cut into workable sections.

Cut the red and almost all of the pink off the rind (a tiny bit of pink looks good!).

Cut the rind into edible, mouth-sized squares or rectangles.

Place chunks into boiling water, reduce heat, wait 3 minutes and remove.

Dissolve canning lime in $1/2$ gallon cool water, add cooled rind and allow to soak refrigerated overnight.

Remove rind from soak, rinse and cover in a pot with fresh water. Bring to a boil and cook until fork tender, about 1 hour; drain and rinse.

Bring vinegar to a boil, add sugar and dissolve, add rind and remaining ingredients except cinnamon sticks. Simmer over low heat for 1 hour, or until syrup is thick. Remove spices in cheesecloth.

Place a cinnamon stick in each jar.

Hot pack by filling with rind chunks and then top off to canning line with syrup according to safe canning practices outlined on page 51.

september

UNLIKE MANY REGIONS of our country, our September does not lose the heat or the humidity of summer. Just the same, the intensity of the sun has lessened, so many farmers have added crops that are now beginning to peek above fresh furrows. This third crop of the year for the same field is one of the reasons Charleston became the self-proclaimed chutney capital. Captains running rice, cotton and indigo to markets in England and Europe sailed the trades. From European ports, following fair winds, their routes took them to South Africa, India, then back around the Cape, up the west coast of Africa and finally across the Atlantic to Jamaica and on to the Carolinas. It is how the first grains of Carolina Gold rice came to this coastal colony. It was a ship's captain giving seed he had collected in Madagascar, in exchange for needed repairs. Chutneys could have happened in any of the frequented ports, but South Carolina just happened to be such a temperate clime. Further south and a hot sun had scorched the land by late spring, while north in Virginia just when Charleston's second and sometimes third crop was coming in, their northern neighbor was getting its first dusting of snow. Pears are the last fruits of a Lowcountry year, so southerners make the most of the crop by sealing the memory of the big canning season with a medley of things "pear."

pear chutney

I have given several chutney recipes, but this is the one most similar to the mango chutney from India and yet was made by colonists using local produce. It is best served with ham or over a block of cream cheese as an hors d'oeuvre.

CANNING NOTES
- **This is a hot pack, acidified recipe.**
- **Initial pH will be below 4.**
- **The recipe makes approximately 96 ounces or 6 pints.**
- **The recipe can be doubled.**

INGREDIENTS
4 pounds pears, any variety but firm fruit, cored, peeled and chopped fine

3 lemons, sliced, seeded and slices quartered

1 1/2 pounds brown sugar

1/4 cup honey

1 1/2 pounds sweet onions, diced

1 quart cider vinegar

3/4 pound light raisins

1/4 pound crystallized ginger, chopped very fine

1 tablespoon mustard seeds

2 teaspoons cayenne pepper (increase amount for a spicier chutney)

2 teaspoons ground cinnamon

1/2 teaspoon ground nutmeg

1/2 teaspoon ground cloves

Prepare and place all ingredients in a pot.

Cook over low boil until mixture thickens and pear chunks are no longer light colored.

Conduct initial pH test. If pH is below 4.3, it is fine. To reduce, add more vinegar 2 tablespoons at a time.

Hot pack above 195 degrees F according to the safe canning practices outlined on page 51.

Perform final pH testing after 24 hours to insure safe canning was accomplished and the pH is below 4.5.

=== kieffer pear ===

There is only one type of pear that grows in the Lowcountry, the Kieffer pear. They are hard as rocks even at their ripest, but the meat is sweet. As a child, when pears began to fall, I had no control over my Tennessee five-gaited walking horse, Lady. She'd get a whiff from the tree and my riding day was over. I would bail off just before she dashed under the limbs to feast. Kieffer pears have a short season and are not grown commercially, yet the season of business is 24/7, so we began using any pear that was available. The softer, more edible, varieties actually make for better relishes and chutney, not to mention the ease of preparation.

pear relish

Relishes made with both fruits and vegetables make for a delightful accompaniment with main courses. When it comes to the simple pork chop, there is suddenly nothing simple about all the complex flavors when enjoined with this relish. It is as if the two were born to be together.

CANNING NOTES
- **This is a hot pack, acidified recipe.**
- **Initial pH will be below 4.**
- **The recipe makes approximately 6 half pints.**
- **The recipe can be doubled.**

INGREDIENTS
3 pounds pears, peeled, seeded and chopped
1 pound red onion, diced
1 large red bell pepper, diced
1¹/₂ cups honey
1¹/₄ cups cider vinegar
³/₄ tablespoon ground cayenne pepper
³/₄ tablespoon cinnamon
2 teaspoons whole mustard seed
1¹/₂ teaspoons turmeric
1 teaspoon ground cloves
1 teaspoon salt

Measure and place all ingredients in a pot and bring to a boil. Reduce heat to medium and cook down until thick.

Conduct initial pH test. If pH is below 4.3, it is fine. To reduce, add more vinegar 1 tablespoon at a time.

Hot pack at 195 degrees F according to the safe canning practices on page 51.

Perform final pH testing after 24 hours to insure safe canning was accomplished and pH is below 4.5

ginger pear preserves

These preserves are lighter in taste than strawberry, peach or fig. They go exceptionally well with brunch dining. Always in the southern dining room of old, the sideboard or table had jars of each preserve from the year's harvests.

CANNING NOTES

- **This is a hot pack, acid recipe.**
- **pH is not an issue. No testing is required.**
- **The recipe makes approximately 6 half pints.**
- **The recipe can be doubled.**

INGREDIENTS

3 pounds pears, firm but ripe, peeled, seeded and chopped
2 pounds sugar
2 lemons, sliced thin, seeded and slices quartered
2 tablespoons lemon juice
2 ounces crystallized ginger, chopped very fine

Place pears and sugar in a pot; simmer, stirring often. When pears are softening, add lemon slices, lemon juice and ginger.

Increase heat and cook until syrup thickens.

Hot pack above 195 degrees F according to safe canning practices outlined on page 51.

corn liquor bbq sauce

When shoppers go to a grocery store and check the ingredients on barbecue sauce labels, they will see one common ingredient—corn syrup. It is added as the sauce sweetener because corn syrup is so sweet less has to be used and, even more to a manufacturer's liking, corn syrup is much less expensive than other sweeteners, even sugar. Read on; it is rare one sees any fresh produce in the ingredients.

In this mix I used the sweeteners of the Old South but, I have to confess, I did use store-bought ketchup. If one truly wants to be a purist, the ketchup recipe is in the June section (see page102). One of my favorite dishes for barbecue sauce is to bake salmon fillets with the sauce painted thickly on top in a 325-degree F oven for just under 30 minutes. Before the salmon goes in, cook up a pot of creamy mixed white and yellow grits (see Resources section). Make grits according to the recipe on the bag. When all is done, ladle a puddle of grits on each plate, plunk the salmon right in the middle and across the top of the fish, width-wise, place spears of either steamed or pickled asparagus. This is simple cooking at its very best.

CANNING NOTES

- **This is a hot pack, acidified recipe.**
- **Initial pH will be below 4.**
- **The recipe makes approximately 90 plus ounces or 5 or more pint jars.**
- **The recipe can be doubled.**

INGREDIENTS

1 cup chopped fine Vidalia onion
2 tablespoons finely minced garlic
$^1/_3$ cup peanut oil
$^1/_2$ cup butter
$^3/_4$ cup diced bell pepper
$2^1/_2$ pounds ketchup
$^3/_4$ cup cider vinegar
$^3/_4$ cup fresh orange juice
$^3/_4$ cup honey
1 cup molasses (non-sulfated)
$^1/_2$ cup Worcestershire sauce
$^1/_4$ cup coarse-ground black pepper
2 tablespoons hot mustard powder (like Colman's)
$^1/_2$ tablespoons salt
$^1/_2$ cup bourbon whiskey, cheap and optional

Sauté onion and garlic in peanut oil and butter until onion is clear. Add balance of ingredients except whiskey. Cook just below boiling until mixture begins to thicken.

Add optional whiskey, stir well and bring to above 200 degrees F.

Conduct initial pH test. If pH is below 4.3, it is fine. To reduce, add more vinegar 2 tablespoons at a time.

Hot pack above 200 degrees F according to safe canning practices outlined on page 51.

Perform final pH testing after 24 hours to insure safe canning was accomplished and the pH is below 4.5.

NOTE: If using traditional barbecue sauce bottles, they will not balance upside down. After sealing, place upside down in the boxes that the bottles came in for the standard 2-minute period.

october

THE YEAR HAS begun to wane. The days are noticeably shorter and the blast furnace that was August and much of September is only a memory. Lowcountry residents have new worries. September and October are peak hurricane months, so with one eye on the weather and the other on the canning calendar we proceed with caution. There is less coming from the fields and many are second crops of earlier produce that we have already pickled. But the pumpkin is a first for the year. Do not pass up the opportunity to work with this special fall symbol. By the last of the month, we will be down to a handful of recipes left to make for the coming holiday seasons.

pumpkin chips

"Chip" is the very colonial Charleston manner of describing hard fruit preserves like pear and apple. The pumpkin chip is about as unique as the Lowcountry itself. Probably first created at Pompion (pronounced Pumpkin or Punkin) Plantation in about 1830, the preserve remained locally popular for the next 120 years. In 1950, the recipe was immortalized when it found its way into the renowned Junior League of Charleston cookbook, now in its thirtieth-plus printing. Many a Lowcountry family still puts up pumpkin chips. So labor intensive is this recipe that one will never find pumpkin chips available in stores. We always made them simply as a labor of love and in an effort to preserve a heritage that dies, a little at a time, with the passing of each generation.

So unique is this preserve that I like giving jars to friends from "off," as the locals say, meaning folks not from the Lowcountry. Thus, I have here a recipe that produces between 8 and 12 pint jars. You adjust the quantity to suit.

CANNING NOTES

- **This is a hot pack, sugar saturated recipe.**
- **pH is not an issue. No testing is required.**
- **The recipe makes about 10 pints or 20 half pints.**
- **The recipe can be doubled.**

With a heavy-blade chef's knife, cut off the top of the pumpkin as if you were making a jack-o-lantern. Do the same with the bottom.

From top to bottom cut 1 1/2-inch-wide slices. Clean and clear the interior side of each slice with a paring knife. Peel outer skin off pumpkin with carrot peeler or knife.

Run slices through a food processor or slice cross-wise in very thin chips. Cut both ends off each lemon and discard; cut lemons in half, juice and reserve both juice and rind.

Remove lemon seeds and chop rind into small chunks and refrigerate.

Place measured chips and sugar in a pot, layering in the two ingredients. Pour lemon juice over the top and mix well. Let stand overnight.

INGREDIENTS

1 medium-sized pumpkin, made into chips (see below)
12 lemons, prepared as described below
1 cup sugar for each 2 cups of chips

Mix well again next day to remove all settled sugar from bottom of pot.

In a small pan filled with water, boil diced lemon rind for 20 minutes; drain well and add to pot.

Bring ingredients to a boil, reduce heat slightly and stir often.

When chips become translucent, remove all from liquid and put aside. Continue to cook liquid.

When liquid begins to thicken but before it darkens, or caramelizes (about 213 degrees F; all water will have left the syrup once the temperature rises above 212 degrees F), return chips to pot.

When boiling resumes, the chips are ready to be canned. Hot pack using a strainer to collect the chips. Fill a jar and then top off with liquid and seal according to safe canning practices outlined on page 51.

sweet potato butter

The sweet potato is a 10,000-year-old Central American, highly nutritious, root vegetable. Many a southern family survived the Civil War (also known as "The Late Unpleasantness") on sweet potatoes. The tubers remained in the ground, unseen by Union forces. Families dug and consumed as needed. In the fall, one begins to see old pickup trucks laden with sweet potatoes parked along the roadside, a scale dangling from the tailgate, their load for sale. The sweet potato's pH is low enough that with the slightest bit of flavorful coaxing, the butter becomes a safe and delicious spread. Apply it to small party sandwiches, as a spread on ham sandwiches or paint on white meats or chicken before cooking. The sweet treat has innumerable possibilities, including use as a pie filling. To make an award-winning sweet potato pie, add 1 egg to a 16-ounce jar of Sweet Potato Butter and fold in thoroughly. Pour the mixture into a half-baked pie shell and sprinkle with brown sugar and pecans. Bake for 20 to 30 minutes in a 350-degree F oven.

CANNING NOTES
- **This is a hot pack, acidified recipe.**
- **Initial pH will be around 4.**
- **The recipe makes approximately 3 pints or 6 half pints.**
- **The recipe can be doubled.**

INGREDIENTS
4 cups sweet potatoes, cooked, peeled and mashed (3 pounds raw potatoes)

$^3/_4$ cup apple juice
1 cup light brown sugar
1 cup white sugar
$^1/_2$ cup orange juice
$^1/_2$ cup lemon juice
$^1/_4$ cup cider vinegar
2 teaspoons cinnamon
1 teaspoon vanilla extract
1 teaspoon salt

Cook potatoes in a 400-degree F oven until soft throughout, about 1 to 1-1/2 hours.

When cool to the touch, peel and purée in a food processor with apple juice until all lumps are gone.

Place all ingredients in a pot and bring to a low boil.

Conduct initial pH test. If pH is below 4.3, it is fine. To reduce, add more cider vinegar, 1 tablespoon at a time.

Hot pack above 200 degrees F according to safe canning practices outlined on page 51.

Perform final pH test after 24 hours to insure a pH below 4.5.

november

NOW BEGINS THE TWO MONTHS that tax a pantry's inventory. There are still a few products to add, but the drain will be far greater than the fill. Pantry management is important. It would be perfect to reach depletion just as next year's crops come on line, but in my home that never seems to happen. It is equally refreshing and encouraging to watch disappointment and desire grow when a canning household runs out between canning seasons. It reminds one that their efforts are not in vain. Farmers are beginning to dig artichokes, but it is best to wait. Fresh out of the ground they have a slightly bitter taste that fades after a month or two of cold storage. So, if out of the preserved goods completely, do a few of the artichoke recipes that are in the February section. The fields now have only greens and edible root plants that enjoy the cooler weather. This will continue well into the winter, however, fresh cranberries are available in every grocery store in early November. My vote is to purchase the freshest of cranberries on the month's first Tuesday while out and about and performing other voting privileges.

cranberry chutney

With the approach of Thanksgiving, it would be nice to add something to the repertoire in the pantry. Everyone is familiar with cranberry jelly and sauce, and some folks find cranberry relish, but when we began creating this chutney we had not heard of anyone producing it. Six years later I see a few brands in stores, but like almost all commercial attempts, the rich flavors the home canner will achieve just aren't there. Making this chutney is as easy as any recipe in this book, takes little time and will be the talk of the Thanksgiving table.

CANNING NOTES
- **This is a hot pack, acid recipe.**
- **pH is not an issue. No testing is required.**
- **This recipe makes 5 or more pints or 11 half pints.**
- **The recipe can be halved or doubled.**

INGREDIENTS

2^1/$_2$ pounds fresh whole cranberries, washed

2 oranges, peeled, sliced and seeded, with slices quartered

1^1/$_4$ ounces garlic cloves, minced

5 cups white sugar

2^1/$_2$ cups cider vinegar

3 ounces crystallized ginger, chopped in blender

^{3}/$_4$ pound light raisins

1^1/$_4$ cups orange juice

1 tablespoon cinnamon

^{1}/$_2$ teaspoons salt

Prepare and place all ingredients in a pot. Bring to boil and reduce heat. Cook for 20 minutes; add water if mixture gets too thick.

Hot pack at 200 degrees F according to safe canning practices outlined on page 51.

mint jelly

With cooler weather and the seasons of entertaining, there might be more red meat consumed. Mint jelly has been a long time staple in pantries, but jelly with the true taste of fresh mint and no silly food coloring is something else entirely. It adds another dimension to chops and legs of lamb and it also works over cream cheese as a party plate.

CANNING NOTES

- **This is a hot pack, sugar saturated recipe.**
- **pH is not an issue. No testing is required.**
- **This recipe makes 6 half pints.**
- **The recipe can be doubled, but not halved.**

INGREDIENTS

$1/2$ **cup chopped fresh mint, packed tight**
$1^1/_2$ **cups cider vinegar**
$1^1/_2$ **cups water**
$6^1/_2$ **cups sugar**
1 pack clear liquid pectin

Bring all ingredients except pectin to a rolling boil in a pot. Add pectin and return to a boil.

Time for $1^1/_2$ minutes and take off the burner.

Hot pack according to safe canning practices outlined on page 51.

— december —

THE CANNING SEASON is over. But with your new canning skills perfected, there is still a chance to shine one last time. If there is ever a month that is filled with entertaining, this is it. It seems like we are still doing Thanksgiving dishes when the doorbell rings and holiday guests are standing at the threshold. If you have followed this canning guide, whether they visit for an evening or for the season, you can regale them with your tasty products. Granted, the peppers might not be as fresh as they are during the summer months, but the bottom half of our globe is enjoying their summer, so good produce can be purchased. I'd rather compromise by using store bought than not having anything for my December festivities.

christmas morning marmalade

This is one of my favorite jars to give as a seasonal gift because it is holiday specific. It is labor intensive—so much so that it needs to be made only once a year.

CANNING NOTES
- **This is a hot pack, acid recipe.**
- **pH is not an issue. No testing is required.**
- **This recipe makes 7 or more pints or 14 half pints.**
- **The recipe can be halved but not doubled.**

INGREDIENTS
$3^1/_2$ ruby red grapefruits, peeled, plugged and seeded (reserve half the rind)
2 thin-skinned oranges, peeled, thin sliced, seeded and quartered (reserve peel)
1 lemon, peeled, thin sliced, seeded and quartered (reserve peel)
4 limes, peeled, $^1/_4$-inch-thick sliced and seeded (reserve peel)
1 cup fresh grapefruit juice
3 cups boiling water
$^1/_8$ teaspoon baking soda
$^1/_2$ tablespoon butter
2 packs powdered pectin
13 cups sugar

Cut saved grapefruit peel in thin strips 1 inch long, removing most white of rind.

Break grapefruit into individual plugs, stripping off tough outer membrane layer of each section; cut skinned plugs in half and place in a pot.

Cut reserved orange, lemon and lime peels into 1-inch-long strips $^1/_{16}$- to $^1/_4$-inch wide.

To a small saucepan with 3 cups boiling water and $^1/_8$ teaspoon baking soda; add lime rind. Reduce heat, simmer 10 minutes, add balance of rinds and simmer an additional 3 minutes.

Add additional water if necessary; drain well, and then add rind to pot with the fruits. Place balance of ingredients except sugar in the pot.

Over high heat, stirring often, bring to a rolling boil. Add half the sugar and return to a boil before adding the balance of the sugar and returning to a third boil. After 2 minutes of boiling, begin testing for jelling. When ready, remove from heat.

Hot pack according to safe canning practices outlined on page 51.

christmas pepper jelly

A lot of the recipes for pepper jellies, especially around Christmas, include red or green food coloring. As far as I'm concerned, these are chemicals and I abhor the use of anything unnatural in canning. So, where we used cider vinegar when we made hot pepper jelly in the summer, we'll now use white vinegar to better bring out the reds and greens of the peppers and we'll add more of both. The end result will be a seasonal look with a fine taste. Your guests will beg for the recipe. Don't give it to them. Suggest that they buy this book, sort of as a Christmas present to me.

CANNING NOTES
- **This is a hot pack, sugar saturated recipe.**
- **pH is not an issue. No testing is required.**
- **This recipe makes 7 plus half pints.**
- **The recipe can be doubled but not halved.**

INGREDIENTS
1^1/$_2$ cups small dice green bell pepper (seeded)
1^1/$_2$ cups small dice red bell pepper (seeded)

1^1/$_2$ cups white vinegar (5 percent acidity)
6^1/$_2$ cups sugar
^{1}/$_2$ tablespoon butter
2 tablespoons red pepper flakes
1 pack liquid pectin (Certo)

Bring all ingredients except pectin to a rolling boil in a pot. Add pectin and return to a boil.

Time for 1^1/$_2$ minutes and begin checking for jelling.

Take pot of burner and begin to hot pack according to safe canning practices outlined on page 51.

field pea relish

For the final canning of the year, this sweet relish is very different from those we have previously put up. From the soul food kitchen on New Year's Day it is said that Hoppin' John and collards bring to the New Year luck and wealth, respectively. This relish provides a complementary accompaniment to the greens and to the peas in the Hoppin' John.

CANNING NOTES
- **This is a hot pack, acidified recipe.**
- **The final pH will be below 4.**
- **The recipe makes 6 pint jars or 12 half pints.**
- **The recipe can be doubled or halved.**

INGREDIENTS
1/4 pound green bell peppers, diced
1/4 pound yellow bell peppers, diced
1/4 pound red bell peppers, diced

1/2 pound red onion, diced
6 cups field peas or cow peas (prepared)
3 ears yellow corn, cut, not scraped, off cob
1/2 tablespoon mustard seed
1/2 teaspoon ground cloves
1/2 teaspoon allspice
1/2 teaspoon curry powder
1/4 teaspoon nutmeg
3 cups white vinegar (5 percent acidity)
1 1/2 pounds sugar

Wash and prepare the produce.

Over medium-high heat, mix all the ingredients in a pot, stirring often until the first sign of boiling.

Conduct initial pH test. If pH is below 4.3, it is fine. To reduce, add more vinegar 2 tablespoons at a time.

Hot pack at 200 degrees F according to safe canning practices outlined on page 51.

Perform final pH test after 24 hours to insure a pH below 4.5.

berry
preserves

— afterthoughts —

When a jar is depleted, wash, inspect for cracks and make sure the sealing edge (i.e. the top of the jar that makes contact with the lid) has remained smooth and is without chips. If it passes muster, store it for the next canning season. The point is, save the empties! The jar and lid are very often equal in price to the ingredients in a jar. Saving the glass will greatly reduce the cost of canning from year to year.

When buying canning jars, the cases generally come accompanied with two-piece lids. The actual lid is a flat, metal disc. It cannot be reused, but once the filled jar has cooled to room temperature, the outer ring may be carefully removed and stored for next years putting up. Boxes of a dozen flat replacement lids are available almost everywhere canning supplies are sold.

If you are going to be using a lot of a non-perishable products, like mustard seed, it pays to order in bulk form. Often a bulk pound of a spice is the same price or even less than a half ounce in a little bottle at the supermarket. In between bulk and the tiny spice jars, stores like Whole Foods sell small tubs of herbs and spices at a fraction of the cost of the smaller quantities.

If you don't grow your own herbs, there might be herb growers in your area. They are in business to supply the food distributors, restaurants and high-end grocers. Get to know them; you'll save a bundle and you'll have access to the finest and freshest herbs at wholesale prices.

Bulk pectin is much less expensive than the pectin sold in little boxes. Consider calling the folks at Pacific Pectin as soon as you become stuck on canning or your family becomes addicted to your preserves.

Many recipes call for red, ripe tomatoes. If the local season has ended and you are still in need, visit a local distributor. He'll have what is called in the trade, "K tomatoes." Ask for "Vine-Ripe K's." These are fruits that are too ripe to send forth. Those folks will probably be more than happy for you to take them off their hands.

Very often we will find ourselves using large quantities of specific products like sugar. Even with a modest canning schedule it will be cost effective to join one of the discount houses like Sam's Club or Costco, or your neighborhood equivalent.

When it comes to purchasing jars, no company I have ever found beats Big Lots. During the season they have large quantities of the most common size jars at the lowest prices. Off season, they do not carry canning jars, so it pays to stock up if you have room to store them.

Rolls of pH paper are less expensive than pH strips. Both accomplish the same task. See where to order pH papers in the Resources section on page 173.

If you intend to purchase a pH meter, you will need calibrating solutions. The powder type that must be mixed with distilled water can be shipped to anyone, but the easy-to-use liquid types are more difficult to ship and are more expensive.

It is important to test after the 24-hour stabilization period, especially for those items with an initial pH above 4.0. This means opening a jar. In the canning section of stores where the jars are located, one will usually find little 4-ounce jelly jars. These make perfect testers and you don't have to break the seal on a bigger jar. This is especially effective when canning quarts of soup.

Very often when canning, there will not be enough left in the pot to fill a final jar. Have a smaller jar standing by. This way, nothing is wasted. Still, if the remainder isn't quite enough to fill a last jar, no problem; seal it and put in the refrigerator for testing and for family use.

GIFT GIVING

I like to use fancy jars for gifts. In the resource section I have included several places where attractive jars can be purchased in other than pallet-sized quantities. When I gift canning jars, I carefully remove the outer rings and cut 4 x 4-inch pieces of calico fabric or a fabric with a seasonal motif. The very enterprising could cut 4-inch-diameter circles. In either case, center the fabric over the jar and gently screw down the outer ring.

I sometimes use a computer and a printer to make a label. At any one of the office supply shops you can purchase #8463 Avery 2"x 4" labels. Once I have completed my year's design, it is easy to change the name of the product, the date canned, ingredients, or anything else you would like on the label. If you do not have a computer, in stores that cater to home canning you can find blank labels to affix to jars. There's nothing wrong with handwriting; it looks more personal than the fanciest printed label.

Here's the really neat thing about giving jars. There's a bunch of money out there, but there isn't a whole lot of time. Thirty years ago I was always hearing that computers would give us more free time to be with our families. What happened? Highways and city streets are now jammed by 6 am. Whatever happened to the family breakfast, or the family supper? People, especially today, really appreciate these home-made gifts and they speak volumes about you. Years ago this was a way of life. It's real easy to run to a store or to go online to order gifts. It takes caring and commitment to do it the old-fashioned way.

resources

Designer Jars
Specialty Bottle
www.specialtybottle.com
206-340-0459

Fillmore Container Inc.
www.fillmorecontainer.com
866-FILL JAR (866-345-5527)

Cape Bottle Co.
www.netbottle.com
888-833-6307

Grits and Canned Products
Specialty Foods South
www.Charlestonfavorites.com
800-538-0003

High-End Kitchen Equipment
Williams-Sonoma
www.williams-sonoma.com

Lowcountry Produce
www.lowcountryproduce.com
800-935-2792

pH Paper and Meters
Science lab.com Inc.
www.sciencelab.com
800-901-7247

Efston Science Inc.
www.efstonscience.com
888-777-5255

Pectin
Pacific Pectin
www.Pacificpectin.com
559-683-0303

Specialty Canning Equipment
Kitchen Krafts
www.kitchenkrafts.com
800-298-5389

Spices
Vann's Spices
www.vannsspices.com
800-583-1693

Metric Conversion Chart

Liquid and Dry Measures

U.S.	Canadian	Australian
¼ teaspoon	1 mL	1 ml
½ teaspoon	2 mL	2 ml
1 teaspoon	5 mL	5 ml
1 tablespoon	15 mL	20 ml
¼ cup	50 mL	60 ml
⅓ cup	75 mL	80 ml
½ cup	125 mL	125 ml
⅔ cup	150 mL	170 ml
¾ cup	175 mL	190 ml
1 cup	250 mL	250 ml
1 quart	1 liter	1 litre

Temperature Conversion Chart

Fahrenheit	Celsius
250	120
275	140
300	150
325	160
350	180
375	190
400	200
425	220
450	230
475	240
500	260

index

A

acidic canning, 59

acidified canning, 42, 59

acidity: chart for, 38–39; understanding, 40–41

altitude, high, 40

alum, 32

apples: Granny Smith, 94; Red Delicious, 127

April canning, 76–79

Artichoke Chow-Chow, 68

Artichoke Pickles, 65

Artichoke Relish, **66**–67

asparagus, pickled, 75

August canning, 135–45

B

bay leaves, removing, 47

beans, black, in Lowcountry Pluff Mud, 57–58

beans, green, in Dilly Beans, 113

beans, lima, in Garden Vegetable Soup, 125

beets, pickled, 79

Blackberry Preserves, 115

blender, 33

blueberries: in Very Berry Preserves, 89

Blueberry Marmalade, 132

Blueberry Preserves, 132

botulism, 40

Bread and Butter Pickles, 84

C

cabbage: in Artichoke Chow-Chow, 68; in Green Tomato Chow-Chow, 83

cabbage, red: in Hot Chow-Chow, 86

canning: meaning of, 18; terminology for, 49; note on, 51, 169; types of, 59

Charleston Creole Sauce, 109

Charleston Gumbo, 110–11

chemicals, canning, 32

chow-chow, 69: artichoke, 68; green tomato, 83; hot, 86

Christmas Morning Marmalade, 164

chutneys: green tomato, 94; red tomato, 101; peach, 123; fruit, 127; Colonial Charleston, 136; pear, 148; cranberry, 160

citric acid, 32

colander, 31

Colonial Charleston Chutney, 136

commercial products, 19–21

cooking pots, 28, 30

cooking terminology, 49

copper pots, 28, 30

Corn Liquor BBQ Sauce, 153

corn: in Garden Vegetable Soup, 125; in Field Pea Relish, 166

cow peas, in Field Pea Relish, 166

Cranberry Chutney, 160

cream cheese and strawberry preserve omelet, 73

cream of asparagus soup, 75

cucumbers: in Uncle Patty's Garlic Pickles, 82; in Bread and Butter Pickles, 84; pickling, 85; in Gazpacho, 100

currants, in Red Tomato Chutney, 101

cutting boards, 28

D

December canning, 163–66

dicing, tips for, 44

Dilled String Beans, **113**–14

doubling recipes, 74

E

enameled pots, 30

equipment, canning, 24–32

F

FDA requirements, 34

February canning, 60–69

Fiery Pickled Garlic, 63

food processor, 33

Fruit Chutney, 127

funnel, canning, 24

G

Garden Vegetable Soup, **124**–25

Garlic Pepper Jelly, 131

Garlic Pickles, 82

Garlic: in Pickled Garlic, 63; in Garlic Pickles, 82; in Garlic Pepper Jelly, 131

Gazpacho, 100

gift giving, 170–71

Ginger Pear Preserves, 151

ginger, crystallized: in Red Tomato Chutney, 101; in Peach Chutney, 123; in Colonial Charleston Chutney, 136; in Pear Chutney, 148; in Ginger Pear

Preserves, 151; in Cranberry
   Chutney
gloves, heat-proof, 33–34
grapefruits, in Christmas
   Morning Marmalade, 164
Green Tomato Chow-Chow, 83
Green Tomato Chutney, 94
Green Tomato Pickle, 86
Green Tomato Relish, 93
Green Tomato Soup, 96

H
herbs: removing, 47;
   purchasing, 169
hors d'oeuvres: Lowcountry
   Pluff Mud, 57–58; Pickled
   Garlic, 63; Artichoke Pickles,
   65; Artichoke Relish, 67;
   Pickled Asparagus, 75;
   Green Tomato Chutney, 94;
   Dilled String Beans, 113;
   Peach Salsa, 121; Peach
   Chutney, 123; Hot Pepper
   Jelly, 129; Garlic Pepper
   Jelly, 131; Okra Pickles, 139
Hot Chow-Chow, 86
hot packing, 35, 59
Hot Pepper Jelly, **128**–29
Hot Pepper Relish, 126
Hot Pickled Garlic, 63

J
jams: tips for, 47; fig, 137
January canning, 55–59
jars, canning, 31–32, 169–70,
   173
jellies: hot pepper, 129; garlic
   pepper, 131; mint, 161;
   Christmas pepper, 165

jelling, 46–47; and doubling
   recipes, 74
Jerusalem artichokes, 64;
   in Artichoke Pickles, 65;
   in Artichoke Relish, 67; in
   Artichoke Chow-Chow, 68;
July canning, 117–33
June canning, 90–115

K
ketchup, tomato, 102
knives, 28

L
lemons: in Strawberry-Orange
   Marmalade, 78; in Blueberry
   Marmalade, 133; in Green
   Tomato Chutney, 94; in Pear
   Chutney, 148; in Ginger Pear
   Preserves, 151; in Pumpkin
   Chips, 156; in Christmas
   Morning Marmalade, 164
lids, canning, 32
lime, canning or slacked, 32
limes, in Christmas Morning
   Marmalade, 164
liquids, reducing, 44
low-acid canning, 59
Lowcountry Pluff Mud, **56**–58

M
mangoes: in Fruit Chutney,
   127; in There's Hot and Then
   There's Hot Sauce, 141
March canning, 70–75
marmalade: strawberry-
   orange, 78; blueberry, 133;
   Christmas Morning, 164
May canning, 80–89

measures, types of, 50
measuring cups, plastic, 26, 28
Mint Jelly, 160

N
November canning, 159–61

O
October canning, 155–57
okra: in Charleston Gumbo,
   111; in Garden Vegetable
   Soup, 125
Okra Pickles, **138**–39
onions, red: in Fruit Chutney,
   127; in Pear Relish, 150; in
   Field Pea Relish, 166
onions, sweet: in Hot Chow-
   Chow, 86; in Green Tomato
   Relish, 93; in Southern
   Tomato Sauce, 97; in Red
   Tomato Relish, 103; in Pear
   Chutney, 148
onions, Vidalia: in Corn Liquor
   BBQ Sauce, 153
onions, white: in Bread and
   Butter Pickles, 84
onions, yellow: in Lowcountry
   Pluff Mud, 57–58; in
   Artichoke Pickles, 65; in
   Artichoke Relish, 67; in
   Artichoke Chow-Chow, 68;
   in Green Tomato Chow-
   Chow, 83; in Green Tomato
   Chutney, 94; in Green
   Tomato Soup, 96; in Tomato
   Salsa, 98; in Red Tomato
   Chutney, 101; in Tomato
   Ketchup, 102; in Seafood
   Cocktail Sauce, 107; in

Charleston Creole Sauce, 109; in Charleston Gumbo, 110–11; in Peach Salsa, 121; in Garden Vegetable Soup, 125; in Pepper Relish, 126; in Colonial Charleston Chutney, 136; in There's Hot and Then There's Hot Sauce, 141

oranges: in Strawberry-Orange Marmalade, 78; in Blueberry Marmalade, 133; in There's Hot and Then There's Hot Sauce, 141; in Cranberry Chutney, 160; in Christmas Morning Marmalade, 164

P

papaya, in Fruit Chutney, 127
Peach Chutney, 123
Peach Cinnamon Preserves, 119
peaches: using, 120; in Colonial Charleston Chutney, 136; in Pickled Peaches, 142
Peach Leather, 143
Peach Mint Preserves, 118
Peach Preserves, 119
Peach Salsa, 121
Pear Chutney, 148
Pear Relish, 150
pears: in Fruit Chutney, 127; Kieffer, 149; in Pear Relish, 151; in Ginger Pear Preserves, 151
Pepper Relish, 126
peppers, green bell:

preparing, 44; in Artichoke Relish, 67; in Artichoke Chow-Chow, 68; in Green Tomato Chow-Chow, 83; in Bread and Butter Pickles, 84; in Southern Tomato Sauce, 97; in Tomato Salsa, 98; in Gazpacho, 100; in Red Tomato Chutney, 101; in Seafood Cocktail Sauce, 107; in Charleston Creole Sauce, 109; in Charleston Gumbo, 110–11; in Peach Salsa, 121; in Pepper Relish, 126; in Fruit Chutney, 127; in Hot Pepper Jelly, 129; in Garlic Pepper Jelly, 131; in Colonial Charleston Chutney, 136; in Corn Liquor BBQ Sauce, 153; in Christmas Pepper Jelly, 165;in Field Pea Relish, 166
peppers, habañero: in Fiery Pickled Garlic, 63; in There's Hot and Then There's Hot Sauce, 141
peppers, hot: preparing, 44–45
peppers, hot red: in Hot Chow–Chow, 86; in Okra Pickles, 139
peppers, jalapeño: in Lowcountry Pluff Mud, 57–58; in Hot Pickled Garlic, 63; in Uncle Patty's Garlic Pickles, 82; in Green Tomato Relish, 93; in Green Tomato Soup, 96; in Charleston Creole Sauce, 109; in Peach Salsa, 121; in Pepper Relish,

126; in Fruit Chutney, 127; in Hot Pepper Jelly, 129; in Garlic Pepper Jelly, 131
peppers, red bell: in Artichoke Pickles, 65; in Artichoke Relish, 67; in Artichoke Chow-Chow, 68; in Hot Chow-Chow, 86; in Green Tomato Relish, 93; in Red Tomato Relish, 103; in Pepper Relish, 126; in Fruit Chutney, 127; in Hot Pepper Jelly, 129; in Garlic Pepper Jelly, 131; in Pear Relish, 150; in Christmas Pepper Jelly, 165; in Field Pea Relish, 166
peppers, yellow bell: in Pepper Relish, 126; in Fruit Chutney, 127; in Field Pea Relish, 166
pH: paper, 33, 170, 173; meter, 34, 170, 173; levels, 39, 41; testing, 42–43
Pickled Asparagus, 75
Pickled Beets, 79
Pickled Garlic, 63
Pickled Peaches, 142
Pickled Shrimp, 106
pickles: Uncle Patty's garlic, 82; Bread and Butter, 98; okra, 139; watermelon rind, 146
pickling, 85
pineapple: in Fruit Chutney, 127
pitchers, measuring, 33
preserves: tips for, 47; strawberry, 73; Very Berry,

89; blackberry, 115; peach mint, 118; peach, 119; blueberry, 133; fig, 137; ginger pear, 151
pressure canning, 19, 59
Pumpkin Chips, 156

R
raisins: in Green Tomato Chutney, 94; in Red Tomato Chutney, 101; in Peach Chutney, 123; in Fruit Chutney, 127; in Colonial Charleston Chutney, 136; in Pear Chutney, 148; in Cranberry Chutney, 160
raspberries: in Very Berry Preserves, 89
Red Tomato Relish, 103
relishes: artichoke, 87; green tomato, 93; red tomato, 102; pepper, 126; hot pepper, 126; pear, 151; field pea, 166

S
salsas: tomato, 98; peach, 121
salt, non-iodized, 32
sauces: Southern Tomato, 97; Seafood Cocktail, 107; Charleston Creole, 109; There's Hot and Then There's Hot, 141; Corn Liquor BBQ, 153
scales, weighing, 24
Seafood Cocktail Sauce, 107
September canning, 147–53
shrimp, 104–5: in Pickled Shrimp, 104; with Seafood Cocktail Sauce, 107; with

Charleston Creole Sauce, 108–9
sodium chloride, 32
sodium hypoclorite, 32, 59
soup: cream of asparagus, 75; green tomato, 96; garden vegetable, 125
Southern Tomato Sauce, 97
spatulas, silicone and metal, 24, 26
stainless steel: pots, 30; removes food odors, 47
sterilization, 38, 59
strawberries: using fresh, 20; in preserves, 73, 89; canning, 74; in marmalade, 78
Strawberry Cinnamon Preserves, 73
Strawberry-Orange Marmalade, 78
Strawberry Preserves, 72–73
sunchokes, 64
Sweet Potato Butter, 157

T
temperature chart: for acidity, 39; for boiling water, 40
There's Hot and Then There's Hot Sauce, 141
thermometer, adjustable cook's, 31, 39–40
Tomato Salsa, 98
tomatoes, green: in Green Tomato Chow-Chow, 83; in Green Tomato Pickle, 87; in Green Tomato Relish, 93; in Green Tomato Chutney, 94; using, 95; in Green Tomato Soup, 96

tomatoes, red: in Hot Chow-Chow, 86; in Southern Tomato Sauce, 97; in Tomato Salsa, 98; using, 99; in Gazpacho, 100; in Red Tomato Chutney, 101; in Tomato Ketchup, 102; in Red Tomato Relish, 103; in Seafood Cocktail Sauce, 107; in Charleston Creole Sauce, 109; in Charleston Gumbo, 110–11; in Peach Salsa, 121; in Garden Vegetable Soup, 125

U
Uncle Patty's Garlic Pickles, 82

V
vacuum sealing, 37, 43
vinegar, 42

W
water bath pot, 30
water bathing, 35, 37, 59
water, distilled, 32
Watermelon Rind Pickles, 145
Whole Fig Preserves and Jam, 137